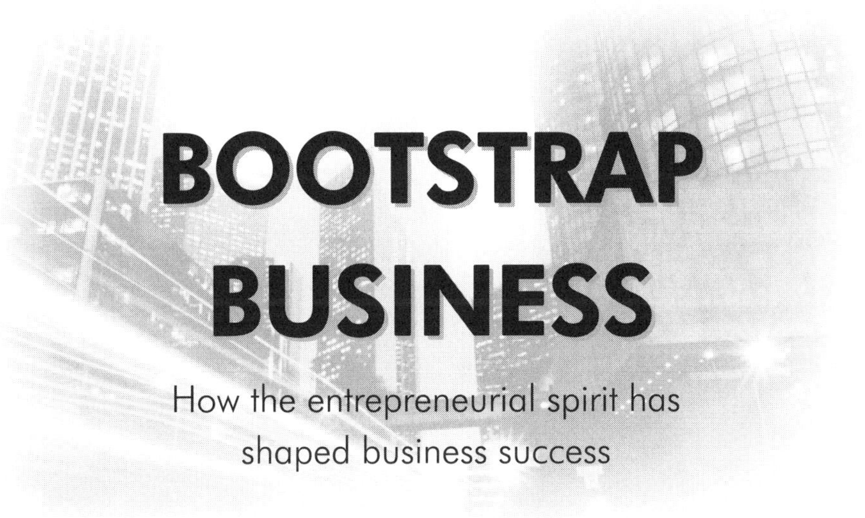

BOOTSTRAP BUSINESS

How the entrepreneurial spirit has shaped business success

Published in the United States by
INSIGHT PUBLISHING COMPANY
647 Wall Street • Sevierville, Tennessee • 37862
www.insightpublishing.com

Disclaimer: This book is a compilation of ideas from numerous experts who have each contributed a chapter. As such, the views expressed in each chapter are of those who were interviewed and not necessarily of the interviewer or Insight Publishing.

10 9 8 7 6 5 4 3 2 1

TABLE OF CONTENTS

A MESSAGE FROM THE PUBLISHER

The interviews found in this book are conducted by David Wright, President of International Speakers Network & Insight Publishing

Being an entrepreneur can be rewarding but is usually a tough endeavor when first starting out. The concept for this book, *Bootstrap Business,* was to gather some people who have succeeded in business and have them share their best advice.

In finding out just what the word "bootstrap" means, as it pertains to business, I found several definitions:

- To promote and develop by use of one's own initiative and work without reliance on outside help
- Undertaken or accomplished with minimal outside help
- Being or relating to a process that is self-initiating or self-sustaining
- By one's own efforts

Those are good definitions but not one person I talked with was able to build his or her business alone. Most of these successful people said that there were many who were influential in helping them build their business. Among these were parents/relatives, mentors, and educators.

When people think of entrepreneurs, they usually think of people who built their businesses without formal education. However, one of our writers said, "Education has played a key role in the development of my businesses and business strategies. It's an essential aspect in developing business skills, it aids in your ability to communicate effectively, how to process information, and how to become a strong leader." I know of some who have had little education but because they listened to successful businesspeople, they were able to put together a business and make it prosper.

Famous speaker, Charlie "Tremendous" Jones, said, "Who we are is a result of the books we read and the people we hang out with." I encourage you to learn the valuable information contained this book. The prosperous people here have given some of the best advice you will ever find about building your business—and your life.

—**David Wright**

CHAPTER ONE

An interview with…

Tod Breslau

From the Ground Up

David Wright (Wright)

Today we're talking with Tod Breslau. Tod is a Portland-based entrepreneur, real estate developer and hospitality icon. He's brought high-energy hospitality to Portland as one of the owners of The Jupiter Hotel. With his hotel, he has realized his dream of a destination that offers travelers a way to experience urban guest lodging within a lively and community-based setting. The Jupiter is part of the new Lobu area of Portland, Oregon, where art, music and humanity cross paths every day. As a native of Philadelphia, his early life centered around entertaining, traveling, and collecting, first for his parent's business and social functions and then for a professional catering firm. After attending the historic Doane Academy in New Jersey, Tod moved to the island of Puerto Rico at age eighteen. There he lived in a mountainside commune, managed a surfside restaurant and bar, and eventually worked for a luxury vacation rental company in San Juan.

During his college career at American University in Washington, D.C., Breslau divided his time working as an intern at the White House as a domestic policy student, working as a student chef for Marriott in the university food services program, and pursuing a degree in economics. He spent half of his last year of college in Madrid studying International Business and Spanish Language Arts. He moved to Los Angeles after graduation to pursue a career in hospitality management and launched Pacific Innovations Restaurant Development Inc. in 1991. As the owner and CEO, he developed Hotel and Free Standing Hospitality Concepts including Cava at the Beverly Plaza Hotel, the Cha Cha Cha Restaurant Chain, and the Mambo Café in San Francisco.

Tod, welcome to *Bootstrap Business*.

Tod Breslau (Breslau)

Good afternoon.

Wright

So when did you first become interested in entrepreneurship and the world of business?

Breslau

I became excited and interested in business at a very young age. As a child, I was fascinated with all aspects of business—how businesses operated, how profits were earned, and the idea of starting from nothing and creating jobs and wealth. From the time I was five years old I spent a lot of time with a family friend whose father owned and operated several restaurants, retail stores and shopping centers. He would share information about his business with me from the time I can remember, where it all began. I had the advantage of spending time looking at his operations, and even from a child's eyes, I was able to begin to decipher how business worked.

Wright

So who were some of the most influential people in your world of coming into business, and how did they affect your career path?

Breslau

Well, let's see; I started out in food and beverage area, specifically in catering as a teenager working the local catering circuit. Beginning in my own family's home, my parents were extensive entertainers and they held endless, large-scale events and parties. They were art collectors and philanthropists and I was able to really see the beginnings of the business back then.

When I moved to Puerto Rico I met a gentleman who owned a restaurant in a seaside town there. He brought me in as an eighteen-year-old working both front and back of the house in the kitchen, restaurant, and bar—I worked in all aspects of the operation. I worked seven days a week, cleaned up, opened up, cooked, bartended, waited tables, and at the end of the day locked up the door and went to the back storeroom to sleep, that's how I started.

From there I went to college in D.C., and I started working for Marriott. Marriott had the food service concession at American University and they handled all the food and beverage facilities at the campus. I got a job right away with them and worked for them throughout my college years. I worked in some of their fast food outlets and then in some of their cafeteria outlets.

After I graduated from college, I moved to Los Angeles and I started working for a renowned restaurant couple who created the famous restaurant chain, Hamburger Hamlet. Both Marilyn and Harry Lewis, the owners and creators of that chain, were an inspiration to me. In 1985, they brought me in as a *maître d'* in one of their top restaurants called Hamlet Gardens. I was trained by a woman who put me through the ringer in the restaurant business. She gave me extensive knowledge on how to run a restaurant, how to hire, how to train, how to improve quality control, and most importantly, to pay attention to customer service, which was critical in my career path as a restaurateur.

Wright

You know, it seems to me that down through the years the word "entrepreneur" almost elicits the feeling that formal education was not a part of it. How does education come into play as far as becoming a successful entrepreneur?

Breslau

Education has played a key role in the development of my businesses and business strategies. It's an essential aspect in developing business skills, it aids in your ability to communicate effectively, how to process information, and how to become a strong leader.

Here's how I looked at it: my college degree was in economics, which on some levels is related to a career in business and entrepreneurship and on many levels, it isn't. What you learn in school, especially in college, is not so much *what* you learn, but as importantly, *how* to learn effectively. I don't think that the educational path you study is as important as the learning process itself—learning how to write, working on group projects, and learning how to listen. These are some key skills that you will pick up in school and transfer to business. Consider all of the papers one writes in college. The exercise of writing an excellent paper in school taught me how to create effective business plans that are instrumental in the projects I have developed over the years. All of those skills came from processing math, writing properly, and many of the various things you learn in college. I think a formal education gives one the foundational skills in being able to negotiate—dealing with investors, dealing with lenders, dealing with landlords, looking at leases—all the things you'll do as an entrepreneur. Some of those skills come through an educational career.

Let me give you another example. When I went to college, I minored in Spanish, because I had lived in Puerto Rico for a couple of years and had a foundation in the language. I studied Spanish at American University for three years, and then I went to Spain and studied at a University in Madrid. When I moved to Los Angeles in 1986, I opened Pacific Innovations Restaurant Development and had seven restaurants operating. I had over one hundred Hispanic employees, all of whom spoke Spanish as their main language. That skill was essential to my being able to work properly with my own employees, which in turn created a sense of mutual respect within my company.

When I became a Real Estate broker in the Portland, Oregon, area, a good portion of my business came from working with Hispanic buyers who were looking for their first house. At the time, it was difficult for Spanish-speaking buyers to find a seasoned agent in the Northwest who was fluent in Spanish, which gave me a competitive advantage. In the end, learning Spanish was one of the most financially rewarding aspects to my educational career, and yet at the time, I was simply studying the language because I enjoyed it.

Wright

I'm glad you shared this part of your experience. I'm going to share this answer with my nineteen-year-old daughter who is in college right now. She's just finished her freshman year. The first thing I told her to do was to take Spanish because 25 percent of the people who are going to be buying and selling will be Hispanics.

Breslau

It's true. In terms of getting a broad education that is well-rounded, diverse, interesting, and fulfilling, I highly recommend to young, future entrepreneurs to take the time and gain a solid education at some point in their career path.

Wright

So what do you consider a successful business, as opposed to an unsuccessful business?

Breslau

Well, I think that as an entrepreneur you must measure, create and gauge your own value—your own scale—as to what you call being successful. Success is different for everyone. I think you need to identify what you want in your life and how you define success for you. It is a combination of the financial success of the business you're involved with and the personal success of your home life, your family life, and your social life. Once you understand your definition of success, then you can start going in that direction.

I think the difference between having a successful business as opposed to an unsuccessful business obviously involves financial success. This means that your business is profitable, you're paying your bills, you're paying your employees, you're creating a product or a service that's gaining momentum and you're doing it with integrity. You're not cutting corners, you're creating value, you're creating jobs, and all the various things that go along with business.

Wright

Would you share with our readers what you believe are the key elements in creating and maintaining a successful business?

Breslau

I think many entrepreneurs would agree that the first element in creating and maintaining a successful business is hard work. If you own a business, whether it's a bakery or a medical sales company or a computer chip company, I think the first thing that we would all agree on is that you, as the owner, the leader, and the entrepreneur, are going to be able to roll up your sleeves, get up first in the morning and be involved in doing the hard work that it's going to take to see this thing through.

Secondly, I think you have to be an effective leader with the company you own. Whether you have two employees, five employees, one hundred employees or a thousand employees, what employees are looking for is a leader who can listen, who can grow with his or her company, who can take good ideas, who can be positive and rewarding to the staff, and build the business's brand and business by empowering employees. I think one of the more successful elements in my businesses is having motivated, talented employees who are treated with respect and whose ideas, talents, and skills are valued and recognized.

Other elements would include financial oversight—making sure that you're not overspending, that you're looking at your bottom line, that you're paying attention to increasing sales, whether it's a service or a product. I've always been a believer in bootstrap business, grassroots marketing and not wasting dollars. For example, at my hotel company (which grosses almost 2.5 million dollars a year) when we print out a piece of paper in the printer, when we don't need it anymore we recycle it and use it again on the other side. We don't like to waste resources. We like to make sure that resources are being maximized. At the end of the day, it's the customer, the guest or the service itself that's getting the proper attention.

Wright

You talked about balance a few minutes ago. How do you balance your personal and professional life, and how do they intertwine?

Breslau

I think it's one thing if you're working nine to five o'clock for a company. Your personal life and your professional life are fairly divided. You get up, get dressed, go to work, go to lunch, go back to work, attend a meeting, and you go home. That's typical in the nine-to-five business world.

When you're an entrepreneur, you have a very different life. You are living and breathing the company you own—the company you operate. The bottom line stops with you, and in any business there is the human factor—people call in sick and people quit, but at the end of the day, the buck stops with you. You have to make sure that things are running smoothly, which means that sometimes you have to get up very early in the morning and you have to work late into the evening. In the hospitality industry it is, in many cases, a twenty-four-hour business. You are responsible for the guest—the end user of your product. You have to make sure that the guest is going to be taken care of. So no matter what, you have to be prepared to be involved with your operation at any given time, and that can interfere with family life.

You have to create balance, and the way to do that is to make sure that you've dotted all your I's and crossed your T's, that you have backup resources for emergency situations, and that you have a way to take some personal time and give your family some of your attention. If all goes well, you can involve your family in your business. They might find it interesting and exciting to be a part of your business. I take my children down to my hotel and let them get a feel for what we're doing there. I share my business conversations, or aspects of them, with my family. I bring my twelve-year-old son to occasional business related events. In general, however, when I come home from work, I leave my business in my briefcase. Family time in our home is important, and I spend a great deal of energy focusing on family time. I am very involved with my children's school—working on committees, volunteering for social and educational events, and coaching on sports teams that my kids participate in. That way, I am ensured a balance from work, quality time with my family, and satisfaction with knowing that I am helping out where I can.

Wright

So what recommendations do you have for people starting up a small business? What are some key steps to raising funds or getting into operation?

Breslau

I tell this to many people because I have several friends and colleagues who come to me with ideas for businesses or questions about the careers that they're in. What has been successful for me in hospitality, in food and beverage, and entertainment, in Real Estate, in the nightclub, and hotel business, has been to become, first and foremost, a sponge.

I started out very young being a sponge in the industry of hospitality. I took on any assignment that any employer would give me. I worked in every capacity in hospitality that I could get my hands on, from dishwasher to general manager. Being a sponge, learning every skill, asking questions, watching, helping, soaking in information is probably the most important element to learning how to start up a business. If you can understand all the nuances of that business, you're going to have a greater chance of being able to develop your own version of it.

When I knew I wanted to go into the restaurant and hospitality business (and I knew that at a pretty young age) I spent ten to fifteen years working for successful operators, being their go-to guy and learning everything I could learn. So when I opened my first restaurant in 1991, I had soaked up many years of knowledge about what it would take to open a restaurant.

After you become a sponge and you have learned about the business and it's time to start that business, you need to raise capital. Typically, with a small business, you will raise funds from either a private source or sources—from what we call "friends and family" investors. You might borrow money from a bank or another lender source. Typically, those lenders are lending money to you as much as they're lending money to your idea.

You will have to be able to create a business plan that is going to impress your financiers and you must be truthful about the product or service that you are creating. You must have the skill to either create that plan yourself or have someone who's an expert at it. In that document you're going to need to show your plan of attack for your business—projected sales and revenues, projected costs, comps from other businesses that are successful in your industry, and a biography and resume information on you and your partners (if there are any). You will have to provide demographics on the area of the business you're going into, which will include customer base, area of the business, and everything else that investors or lenders are going to require to prove your business is viable and that you are trustworthy.

Those are key elements to starting a business, and that's why education—learning how to write and understanding language and math—is an important part of being an entrepreneur.

Once you have the funds you need, then it's time to get started. This is a matter of what I call modeling, and that means going to the experts. If you're looking for a location for your business, you go to the top brokers in the area—you go to other people who already have similar businesses but who are not in a competitive area. You ask questions, you ask for help, and you ask mentors to help you get started.

Wright

So what are some of the exciting fields of entrepreneurship that are available to newcomers in business today?

Breslau

Well, I think there is a huge amount of demand for anything that has to do with the elderly. We are coming into that time when Baby Boomers are aging rapidly. The segment of the population over fifty is massive and the amount of dollars they have to spend is extensive. So if you're looking for a business that deals with services and semi-medical or therapeutic business for the elderly, I think these are fields that have endless opportunities. Senior living is virtually untapped in terms of creative and innovative housing and services for the elderly.

The business that I'm in, which is the business of budget boutique hospitality, is also on a growth pattern, especially with the higher cost of fuel and food. Savings on hotels will be a key factor in the decision-making of corporate travel planners.

Healthy, alternative fast food, snacks, and beverages are still in growth stages. Fast food has not evolved very much in the last fifty years. A hamburger is still pretty greasy in most fast food places, and the demand for healthy fast food hasn't really been addressed.

Alternative energy businesses, including biofuel, solar, wind, and electric vehicles, are really still just beginning to blossom, and there will be a growing demand for people in sales, marketing and engineering in all of the various energy industries that are evolving. I think there are going to be hundreds of thousands of jobs and related services in alternative energy. For example, I have a friend who goes to fast food restaurants to get their old French fry oil (they do not charge him for it). He takes it home to his garage and makes biofuel for his diesel car. His net cost is around seventy-five cents per gallon.

A few months ago, I was reading an article about a company that is now buying the old oil from every restaurant that it can to create biofuel to resell. Think about it. When I was in the restaurant business in the 1990s, we used to pay a company to come and pick up our used oil. Now, companies are paying restaurants for that same old oil, converting it to fuel, and reselling it. Expand that nationally, and you have a whole new industry.

Wright

So what is the reason that you most often give as to why and how you became a successful entrepreneur?

Breslau

I think some of the key reasons that have helped me become a success in business are as follows:

Creativity. I think I've been blessed with a gene of creativity that has helped me come up with solutions in various situations in business that have helped me with my career. Creativity has helped me answer questions, deal with challenges, deal with employee issues, sales issues, financial issues, and more. When something comes up that needs to be tackled (and it always does), having a creative solution can be critical. That's probably been one of my really successful value points. So if you're looking at becoming an entrepreneur, a business leader, and an employer, really try to hone your creative skills.

Read. Read everything you can get your hands on that is related to your field. I've read many books on the subjects of hospitality, food and beverage, management, marketing, sales, real estate, finance, customer service, and more. *I've read countless volumes* on success, wealth building, positive motivation and employee relations.

Flexibility. Being a flexible leader and being a flexible businessperson can be a key factor in negotiating the turmoil of growing a business. You're going to wake up one day of every week and there's going to be a freight train coming at you (in the hospitality business there are twenty freight trains a day that come our way). As an entrepreneur, being flexible with how you're going to tackle those issues, how you are going to sidestep that train, and how you're going to make sure your customers are happy in the end is a key element in being successful. It really boils down to being flexible and understanding that, even though you thought it was going to be a certain way, it might have to be a different way, and you're going to be ready for that.

Be thorough. Being thorough in business means that when you're working on a project or a business or a start-up or a company, and there are times that come along where you feel like you're worn out and you've just given all you can, chances are you've got to give another 110 percent beyond that. You have to be thorough, and this means that if you're in the restaurant business and all your employees have gone home, you still walk through the property and make sure the lights are turned off, the tables are clean, the deep fryer's been wiped out—you have to be thorough. If you haven't done that, when you come in the next day and there's a problem that you've created for the next guy, then that's going to come right back at you.

Those are the elements that I think are important to becoming a successful entrepreneur.

Wright

So what's next for Tod Breslau? Where do you see yourself going from here, and how will you get there?

Breslau

Currently I am working on an expansion of our very successful hotel brand, The Jupiter Hotel. This is a hospitality concept that we designed back in 2001. We are entering our fifth year of business, and we're very excited about the possibility of expanding to other markets. We are in the process of sourcing new locations nationally, looking for investors, additional team members, and finance partners so that we can create additional hotels in various urban markets.

How will we get there? We will get there by continuing to hit home runs with the properties that we are developing, just as we have with our first property. We're paying great returns to our investment pool, our team is managing our property successfully and we are looking for key locations in various cities. The Jupiter Hotel was named one of the top boutique hotels of 2005 by *GQ Magazine*. *Condé Nast Traveler Magazine* put us on their top one hundred list, and various other publications have given us accolades that have helped customers see that we are an exciting alternative to a Holiday Inn or a Doubletree or a Hyatt.

Wright

Well, I wish you the very best in all of those endeavors. It sounds as though you already know how to get there.

I really appreciate all the time you've taken to answer these questions, Tod. You've given me a lot to think about and I am certain that our readers are going to be fascinated and helped by this information.

Breslau

Thank you for inviting me to share my ideas with your readers.

Wright

Today we're talking with Tod Breslau. In 2001, he began purchasing and developing various residential and commercial properties including the Jupiter Hotel property located in the up and coming Lobu neighborhood of Portland, Oregon. The Jupiter was named one of the top hotels in the *Condé Nast Traveler Magazine* (2005) and *GQ Magazine*. *The Jupiter Hotel* offers travelers to Portland a combination of high design, style and low budget hospitality in addition to incredible nightclub and dining experiences at the on-site Doug Fir Lounge. Tod divides his time between the Jupiter Hotel and his brokerage firm, Windermere Community Realty, a residential and commercial Real Estate brokerage in Portland. His work in Real Estate has earned him the Diamond Platinum Broker of the Portland Metropolitan Association of Realtors and he has been ranked in the top 10 percent of all Portland Real Estate brokers.

Tod, thank you so much for being with us today on *Bootstrap Business.*

Breslau

Thank you.

ABOUT THE AUTHOR

Tod Breslau is the creator and co-founder of the Jupiter Hotel in Portland, Oregon, in 2002. He conceived, designed and created the renowned Jupiter Hotel (www.jupiterhotel.com). Tod began his hospitality career in the 1980s as the Executive Director of the Stock Exchange Nightclub, to be followed by the Director of Marketing for Vertigo Nightclub. These two top Los Angeles mega clubs helped launch Breslau's career as a hospitality icon. Following the club years, Breslau launched Pacific Innovations Hospitality Group, which included the development of Cha Cha Cha Restaurants, Hollywood; Silverlake, La Jolla, Long Beach; Cha Cha Chicken in Santa Monica; CAVA Supper Club at the Beverly Plaza Hotel, Ivy at the Waterfront Hotel in Scottsdale, design consulting at the Namale Resort in Fiji, and the Mambo Café in San Francisco.

After moving to Portland, Oregon, in 1998, Breslau launched a custom interior design business (www.huntgather.com and www.sofatablechair.com). The interiors businesses focused on creating custom case-good furniture for both residential and commercial applications. In 2002, Breslau sold the Interiors studios and launched the Jupiter Hotel brand, developing the real estate, the concept, logos, brand, management team, interior and exterior design, marketing and public relations strategies and overall concept of this award winning budget boutique hotel.

Breslau is a commercial and residential Real Estate broker and developer and a senior multi-million dollar producer at Equity Builders Realty, Portland, and has brokered over $30,000,000 in real estate transactions since 2002.

Tod Breslau

1901 NE Broadway
Portland, OR
503.740.4888
tbreslau@aol.com
www.jupiterhotel.com

CHAPTER TWO

An interview with...

Jack Canfield

Decide What You Want and Do What it Takes

David Wright (Wright)

Today we are talking with Jack Canfield. You probably know him as the founder and co-creator of the *New York Times* number one bestselling *Chicken Soup for the Soul* book series. As of 2006, there are sixty-five titles and eighty million copies in print in over thirty-seven languages.

Jack's background includes a BA from Harvard, a master's from the University of Massachusetts, and an Honorary Doctorate from the University of Santa Monica. He has been a high school and university teacher, a workshop facilitator, a psychotherapist and a leading authority in the area of self-esteem and personal development.

Jack Canfield, welcome to *Bootstrap Business*.

Jack Canfield (Canfield)

Thank you, David. It's great to be with you.

Wright

I talked with Mark Victor Hansen a few days ago. He gave you full credit for coming up with the idea of the *Chicken Soup* series. Obviously, it's made you an internationally known personality. Other than recognition, has the series changed you personally and if so, how?

Canfield

I would say that it has and I think in a couple of ways. Number one, I read stories all day long of people who've overcome what would feel like insurmountable obstacles. For example, we just did a book *Chicken Soup for the Unsinkable Soul.* There's a story in there about a single mother with three daughters. She contracted a disease and she had to have both of her hands and both of her feet amputated. She got prosthetic devices and was able to learn how to use them. She could cook, drive the car, brush her daughters' hair, get a job, etc. I read that and I thought, "God, what would I ever have to complain and whine and moan about?"

At one level, it's just given me a great sense of gratitude and appreciation for everything I have and it has made me less irritable about the little things.

I think the other thing that's happened for me personally is my sphere of influence has changed. By that, I mean I was asked, for example, a couple of years ago to be the keynote speaker to the Women's Congressional Caucus. The Caucus is a group that includes all women in America who are members of Congress and who are state senators, governors and lieutenant governors. I asked what they wanted me to talk about—what topic.

"Whatever you think we need to know to be better legislators," was the reply.

I thought, "Wow, they want me to tell them about what laws they should be making and what would make a better culture." Well, that wouldn't have happened if our books hadn't come out and I hadn't become famous. I think I get to play with people at a higher level and have more influence in the world. That's important to me because my life purpose is inspiring and empowering people to live their highest vision so the world works for everybody. I get to do that on a much bigger level than when I was just a high school teacher back in Chicago.

Wright

I think one of the powerful components of that book series is that you can read a positive story in just a few minutes and come back and revisit it. I know my daughter has three of the books and she just reads them interchangeably. Sometimes I go in her bedroom and she'll be crying and reading one of them. Other times she'll be laughing, so they really are "chicken soup for the soul," aren't they?

Canfield

They really are. In fact, we have four books in the *Teenage Soul* series now and a new one coming out at the end of this year. I have a son who's eleven and he has a twelve-year-old friend who's a girl. We have a new book called *Chicken Soup for the Teenage Soul and the Tough Stuff.* It's all about dealing with parents' divorces, teachers who don't understand you, boyfriends who drink and drive, and other issues pertinent to that age group.

I asked my son's friend, "Why do you like this book?" (It's our most popular book among teens right now.) She said, "You know, whenever I'm feeling down I read it and it makes me cry and I feel better. Some of the stories make me laugh and some of the stories make me feel more responsible for my life. But basically I just feel like I'm not alone."

One of the people I work with recently said that the books are like a support group between the covers of a book—you can read about other peoples' experiences and realize you're not the only one going through something.

Wright

Jack, we're trying to encourage people in our audience to be better, to live better and be more fulfilled by reading about the experiences of our writers. Is there anyone or anything in your life that has made a difference for you and helped you to become a better person?

Canfield

Yes, and we could do ten books just on that. People influence me all the time. If I were to go way back, I'd have to say one of the key influences in my life was Jesse Jackson when he was still a minister in Chicago. I was teaching in an all black high school there and I went to Jesse Jackson's church with a friend one time. What happened for me was that I saw somebody with a vision. (This was before Martin Luther King was killed and Jesse was of the lieutenants in his organization.) I just saw people trying to make the world work better for a certain segment of the population. I was inspired by that kind of visionary belief that it's possible to make change.

Later on, John F. Kennedy was a hero of mine. I was very much inspired by him.

Another is a therapist by the name of Robert Resnick. He was my therapist for two years. He taught me a little formula: E + R = O. It stands for Events + Response = Outcome. He said, "If you don't like your outcomes quit blaming the events and start changing your responses." One of his favorite phrases was, "If the grass on the other side of the fence looks greener, start watering your own lawn more."

I think he helped me get off any kind of self-pity I might have had because I had parents who were alcoholics. It would have been very easy to blame them for problems I might have had. They weren't very successful or rich; I was surrounded by people who were and I felt like, "God, what if I'd had parents like they had? I could have been a lot better." He just got me off that whole notion and made me realize that the hand you were dealt is the hand you've got to play. Take responsibility for who you are and quit complaining and blaming others and get on with your life. That was a turning point for me.

I'd say the last person who really affected me big-time was a guy named W. Clement Stone who was a self-made multi-millionaire in Chicago. He taught me that success is not a four-letter word—it's nothing to be ashamed of—and you ought to go for it. He said, "The best thing you can do for the poor is not be one of them." Be a model for what it is to live a successful life. So I learned from him the principles of success and that's what I've been teaching now for more than thirty years.

Wright

He was an entrepreneur in the insurance industry, wasn't he?

Canfield

He was. He had combined insurance. When I worked for him he was worth 600 million dollars and that was before the dot.com millionaires came along in Silicon Valley. He just knew more about success. He was a good friend of Napoleon Hill (author of *Think and Grow Rich)* and he was a fabulous mentor. I really learned a lot from him.

Wright

I miss some of the men I listened to when I was a young salesman coming up and he was one of them. Napoleon Hill was another one as was Dr. Peale. All of their writings made me who I am today. I'm glad I had that opportunity.

Canfield

One speaker whose name you probably will remember is Charlie "Tremendous" Jones. He passed away in October 2008 and he is greatly missed. He said, "Who we are is a result of the books we read and the people we hang out with." I think that's so true and that's why I tell people, "If you want to have high self-esteem, hang out with people who have high self-esteem. If you want to be more spiritual, hang out with spiritual people." We're always telling our children, "Don't hang out with those kids." The reason we don't want them to is because we know how influential people are with each other. I think we need to give ourselves the same advice. Who are we hanging out with? We can hang out with them in books, cassette tapes, CDs, radio shows, and in person.

Wright

One of my favorites was a fellow named Bill Gove from Florida. I talked with him about three or four years ago. He's retired now. His mind is still as quick as it ever was. I thought he was one of the greatest speakers I had ever heard.

What do you think makes up a great mentor? In other words, are there characteristics that mentors seem to have in common?

Canfield

I think there are two obvious ones. I think mentors have to have the time to do it and the willingness to do it. I also think they need to be people who are doing something you want to do. W. Clement Stone used to tell me, "If you want to be rich, hang out with rich people. Watch what they do, eat what they eat, dress the way they dress—try it on." He wasn't suggesting that you give up your authentic self, but he was pointing out that rich people probably have habits that you don't have and you should study them.

I always ask salespeople in an organization, "Who are the top two or three in your organization?" I tell them to start taking them out to lunch and dinner and for a drink and finding out what they do. Ask them, "What's your secret?" Nine times out of ten they'll be willing to tell you.

This goes back to what we said earlier about asking. I'll go into corporations and I'll say, "Who are the top ten people?" They'll all tell me and I'll say, "Did you ever ask them what they do different than you?"

"No," they'll reply.

"Why not?"

"Well, they might not want to tell me."

"How do you know? Did you ever ask them? All they can do is say no. You'll be no worse off than you are now."

So I think with mentors you just look at people who seem to be living the life you want to live and achieving the results you want to achieve.

What we say in our book is when that you approach a mentor they're probably busy and successful and so they haven't got a lot of time. Just ask, "Can I talk to you for ten minutes every month?" If I know it's only going to be ten minutes I'll probably say yes. The neat thing is if I like you I'll always give you more than ten minutes, but that ten minutes gets you in the door.

Wright

In the future are there any more Jack Canfield books authored singularly?

Canfield

One of my books includes the formula I mentioned earlier: E + R = O. I just felt I wanted to get that out there because every time I give a speech and I talk about that the whole room gets so quiet you could hear a pin drop—I can tell people are really getting value.

Then I'm going to do a series of books on the principles of success. I've got about 150 of them that I've identified over the years. I have a book down the road I want to do that's called *No More Put-Downs,* which is a book probably aimed mostly at parents, teachers, and managers. There's a culture we have now of put-down humor. Whether it's *Married . . . with Children* or *All in the Family,* there's that characteristic of macho put-down humor. There's research now showing how bad it is for kids' self-esteem when the coaches do it, so I want to get that message out there as well.

Wright

It's really not that funny, is it?

Canfield

No, we'll laugh it off because we don't want to look like we're a wimp but underneath we're hurt. The research now shows that you're better off breaking a child's bones than you are breaking their spirit. A bone will heal much more quickly than their emotional spirit will.

Wright

I remember recently reading a survey where people listed the top five people who had influenced them. I've tried it on a couple of groups at church and in other places. In my case, and in the survey, approximately three out of the top five are always teachers. I wonder if that's going to be the same in the next decade.

Canfield

I think that's probably because as children we're at our most formative years. We actually spend more time with our teachers than we do with our parents. Research shows that the average parent only interacts verbally with each of their children only about eight and a half minutes a day. Yet at school they're interacting with their teachers for anywhere from six to eight hours depending on how long the school day is, including coaches, chorus directors, etc.

I think that in almost everybody's life there's been that one teacher who loved him or her as a human being—an individual—not just one of the many students the teacher was supposed to fill full of History and English. That teacher believed in you and inspired you.

Les Brown is one of the great motivational speakers in the world. If it hadn't been for one teacher who said, "I think you can do more than be in a special education class. I think you're the one," he'd probably still be cutting grass in the median strip of the highways in Florida instead of being a $35,000-a-talk speaker.

Wright

I had a conversation one time with Les. He told me about this wonderful teacher who discovered Les was dyslexic. Everybody else called him dumb and this one lady just took him under her wing and had him tested. His entire life changed because of her interest in him.

Canfield

I'm on the board of advisors of the Dyslexic Awareness Resource Center here in Santa Barbara. The reason is because I taught high school and had a lot of kids who were called "at-risk"—kids who would end up in gangs and so forth.

What we found over and over was that about 78 percent of all the kids in the juvenile detention centers in Chicago were kids who had learning disabilities—primarily dyslexia—but there were others as well. They were never diagnosed and they weren't doing well in school so they'd drop out. As soon as a student drops out of school he or she becomes subject to the influence of gangs and other kinds of criminal and drug linked activities. If these kids had been diagnosed earlier we'd have been able to get rid of a large amount of the juvenile crime in America because there are a lot of really good programs that can teach dyslexics to read and excel in school.

Wright

My wife is a teacher and she brings home stories that are heartbreaking about parents not being as concerned with their children as they used to be, or at least not as helpful as they used to be. Did you find that to be a problem when you were teaching?

Canfield

It depends on what kind of district you're in. If it's a poor district the parents could be on drugs, alcoholics, and basically just not available. If you're in a really high rent district the parents are not available because they're both working, coming home tired, they're jet-setters, or they're working late at the office because they're workaholics. Sometimes it just legitimately takes two paychecks to pay the rent anymore.

I find that the majority of parents care but often they don't know what to do. They don't know how to discipline their children. They don't know how to help them with their homework. They can't pass on skills that they never acquired themselves.

Unfortunately, the trend tends to be like a chain letter. The people with the least amount of skills tend to have the most number of children. The other thing is that you get crack babies (infants born addicted to crack cocaine because of the mother's addiction). As of this writing, in Los Angeles one out of every ten babies born is a crack baby.

Wright

That's unbelievable.

Canfield

Yes, and another statistic is that by the time 50 percent of the kids are twelve years old they have started experimenting with alcohol. I see a lot of that in the Bible belt. The problem is not the big city, urban designer drugs, but alcoholism.

Another thing you get, unfortunately, is a lot of let's call it "familial violence"—kids getting beat up, parents who drink and then explode, child abuse, and sexual abuse. You see a lot of that.

Wright

Most people are fascinated by these television shows about being a survivor. What has been the greatest comeback that you have made from adversity in your career or in your life?

Canfield

You know, it's funny, I don't think I've had a lot of major failures and setbacks where I had to start over. My life's been on an intentional curve. But I do have a lot of challenges. Mark and I are always setting goals that challenge us. We always say, "The purpose of setting a really big goal is not so that you can achieve it so much, but it's who you become in the process of achieving it." A friend of mine, Jim Rohn, says, "You want to set goals big enough so that in the process of achieving them you become someone worth being."

I think that to be a millionaire is nice but so what? People make the money and then they lose it. People get the big houses and then they burn down or Silicon Valley goes belly up and all of a sudden they don't have a big house anymore. But who you became in the process of learning how to be successful can never be taken away from you. So what we do is constantly put big challenges in front of us.

We have a book called *Chicken Soup for the Teacher's Soul.* (You'll have to make sure to get a copy for your wife.) I was a teacher and a teacher trainer for years. But because of the success of the *Chicken Soup* books I haven't been in the education world that much. I've got to go out and relearn how I market to that world. I met with a Superintendent of Schools. I met with a guy named Jason Dorsey who's one of the number one consultants in the world in that area. I found out who has the bestselling book in that area. I sat down with his wife for a day and talked about her marketing approaches.

I believe that if you face any kind of adversity, whether it's losing your job, your spouse dies, you get divorced, you're in an accident like Christopher Reeve and become paralyzed, or whatever, you simply do what you have to do. You find out who's already handled the problem and how did they've handled it. Then you get the support you need to get through it by their example. Whether it's a counselor in your church or you go on a retreat or you read the Bible, you do something that gives you the support you need to get to the other end.

You also have to know what the end is that you want to have. Do you want to be remarried? Do you just want to have a job and be a single mom? What is it? If you reach out and ask for support I think you'll get help. People really like to help other people. They're not always available because sometimes they're going through problems also; but there's always someone with a helping hand.

Often I think we let our pride get in the way. We let our stubbornness get in the way. We let our belief in how the world should be interfere and get in our way instead of dealing with how the world is. When we get that out of that way then we can start doing that which we need to do to get where we need to go.

Wright

If you could have a platform and tell our audience something you feel that would help or encourage them, what would you say?

Canfield

I'd say number one is to believe in yourself, believe in your dreams, and trust your feelings. I think too many people are trained wrong when they're little kids. For example, when kids are mad at their daddy they're told, "You're not mad at your Daddy."

They say, "Gee, I thought I was."

Or the kid says, "That's going to hurt," and the doctor says, "No it's not." Then they give you the shot and it hurts. They say, "See that didn't hurt, did it?" When that happened to you as a kid, you started to not trust yourself.

You may have asked your mom, "Are you upset?" and she says, "No," but she really was. So you stop learning to trust your perception.

I tell this story over and over. There are hundreds of people I've met who've come from upper class families where they make big incomes and the dad's a doctor. The kid wants to be a mechanic and work in an auto shop because that's what he loves. The family says, "That's beneath us. You can't do that." So the kid ends up being an anesthesiologist killing three people because he's not paying attention. What he really wants to do is tinker with cars.

I tell people you've got to trust your own feelings, your own motivations, what turns you on, what you want to do, what makes you feel good, and quit worrying about what other people say, think, and want for you. Decide what you want for yourself and then do what you need to do to go about getting it. It takes work.

I read a book a week minimum and at the end of the year I've read fifty-two books. We're talking about professional books—books on self-help, finances, psychology, parenting, and so forth. At the end of ten years I've read 520 books. That puts me in the top 1 percent of people knowing important information in this country. But most people are spending their time watching television.

When I went to work for W. Clement Stone, he told me, "I want you to cut out one hour a day of television."

"Okay," I said, "what do I do with it?"

"Read," he said.

He told me what kind of books to read. He said, "At the end of a year you'll have spent 365 hours reading. Divide that by a forty-hour work week and that's nine and a half weeks of education every year."

I thought, "Wow, that's two months." It was like going back to summer school.

As a result of his advice I have close to 8,000 books in my library. The reason I'm involved in this book project instead of someone else is that people like me, Jim Rohn, Les Brown, and you read a lot. We listen to tapes and we go to seminars. That's why we're the people with the information.

I always say that your raise becomes effective when you do. You'll become more effective as you gain more skills, more insight, and more knowledge.

Wright

Jack, I have watched your career for over a decade and your accomplishments are just outstanding. But your humanitarian efforts are really what impress me. I think that you're doing great things not only in California, but all over the country.

Canfield

It's true. In addition to all of the work we do, we pick one to three charities and we've given away over six million dollars in the last eight years, along with our publisher who matches every penny we give away. We've planted over a million trees in Yosemite National Park. We've bought hundreds of thousands of cataract operations in third world countries. We've contributed to the Red Cross, the

Humane Society, and on it goes. It feels like a real blessing to be able to make that kind of a contribution to the world.

Wright

Today we have been talking with Jack Canfield, founder and co-creator of the Chicken Soup for the Soul book series.

Canfield

Another book is *The Success Principles*. In it I share sixty-four principles that other people and I have utilized to achieve great levels of success.

In 2002, we published *Chicken Soup for the Soul of America*. It includes stories that grew out of 9/11 and is a real healing book for our nation. I would encourage readers to get a copy and share it with their families.

Wright

I will stand in line to get one of those. Thank you so much being with us.

ABOUT THE AUTHOR

Jack Canfield is one of America's leading experts on developing self-esteem and peak performance. A dynamic and entertaining speaker, as well as a highly sought-after trainer, he has a wonderful ability to inform and inspire audiences toward developing their own human potential and personal effectiveness.

Jack Canfield is most well-known for the *Chicken Soup for the Soul* series, which he co-authored with Mark Victor Hansen, and for his audio programs about building high self-esteem. Jack is the founder of Self-Esteem Seminars, located in Santa Barbara, California, which trains entrepreneurs, educators, corporate leaders, and employees how to accelerate the achievement of their personal and professional goals. Jack is also founder of The Foundation for Self Esteem, located in Culver City, California, which provides self-esteem resources and training to social workers, welfare recipients, and human resource professionals.

Jack graduated from Harvard in 1966, received his ME degree at the University of Massachusetts in 1973, and earned an Honorary Doctorate from the University of Santa Monica. He has been a high school and university teacher, a workshop facilitator, a psychotherapist, and a leading authority in the area of self-esteem and personal development.

As a result of his work with prisoners, welfare recipients, and inner-city youth, Jack was appointed by the State Legislature to the California Task Force to Promote Self-Esteem and Personal and Social Responsibility. He also served on the Board of Trustees of the National Council for Self-Esteem.

Jack Canfield

The Jack Canfield Companies
Phone: 805.563.2935
www.jackcanfield.com

CHAPTER THREE

An interview with...

Heather Christie

Strategic Streamlining—Are You Getting the Results You Want from Your Planning Process?

David Wright (Wright)

Today we're talking with Heather Christie who is a Franchisor for ActionCOACH Business Coaching in the State of Florida and Co-Founder and Chairman of the ActionCOACH Business Coaching Firm in Southwest Florida. With over twenty years of business and legal experience, Heather is a professional business advisor, attorney, and professional public speaker.

As a certified Business and Executive Coach and Trainer, she was recently elected by over one thousand of her peers to receive the Global Coach's Choice Award, which is given each year to the top coach in the ActionCOACH Organization. She works primarily with midsized privately held companies to improve performance—from executive retreats to implementation of her proprietary Strategic Streamlining methodology. Heather brings a fresh and simple approach to organizations that are tired of missing their budget.

We are fortunate to have her as a contributing author for our chapter on Strategic Streamlining to share with us her expertise on her results-focused planning methodology. She has a unique background as a professional business advisor, a former partner at a prominent Chicago law firm, and a Certified Business and Executive Coach. Heather has spent the last fifteen years consulting with all levels of businesses from privately held companies to Fortune 50 executives. Her system is called V-CAAR™ and is nothing short of revolutionary for companies.

Heather, welcome to *Bootstrap Business.*

So what are some of the top challenges that you are hearing from business owners and executives these days?

Heather Christie (Christie)

The top challenges can basically be summarized into three categories: time, team, and money. Each of those three categories really relate back to one more fundamental business issue, which is lack of focus, clarity, or what you might call a rock solid plan. Planning is one of those activities in business that many people might think of as a necessary evil, yet when executives get really good at using a simple methodology, life and business become a whole lot easier.

Wright

I mentioned in your introduction, your "Strategic Streamlining" system called V-CAAR. Would you tell our readers about V-CAAR?

Christie

V-CAAR is a five-step planning methodology that business owners can use to streamline their plan and results. It's an updated integrative planning process loosely based on a methodology originally documented by George Morrisey, Patrick Below, and Betty Acomb back in the eighties. The acronym stands for:

Variance
Cause
Action Plan
Accountability
Re-forecasting for Results

I will be describing this in more detail later.

Wright

Variance, Cause, Action Plan, Accountability, and Re-forecasting for Results. Okay, so how does your system differ from traditional planning methodologies?

Christie

Traditional planning methodologies tend to involve long-term, strategic planning and short-term, operational planning. Rarely does traditional planning include a formal process of results management, which is where the rubber really meets the road. When it comes to "planning," the extremes go from no planning with lots of reactive activity, to over planning without implementation.

What we find overall is that most companies fall somewhere in between those two extremes. They plan using methodologies that they have learned throughout their careers, which usually is something in the form of getting from A to B, by when. They identify the person responsible for accomplishing the task, and assign a deadline. So if you look at that as a somewhat traditional methodology, our process takes planning to the next level of integrating Strategic Streamlining with operational planning and includes integrated accountability through measuring results on a continuing monthly basis.

The V-CAAR System can be described as follows: for every plan that is created there's always going to be a Variance at some level, and it can be either up or down and it can be in revenue and/or expenses. Once you have identified the variance, then you want to examine the Cause for that variance. I think executives often recognize the variance, but they don't always dig deep enough to really analyze what caused that variance. Identifying the cause for that variance then allows us to come up with operational Action Plans—the actions needed to be taken based on the cause analysis. Once we find out the actions necessary, then we determine who in the organization is Accountable for executing those actions.

Then the last and most critical piece of V-CAAR is the Re-forecasting for Results. This is where the executive team reviews the original budget against the actuals on a monthly basis. All budgets are created using assumptions before the year even begins that are based on the best information available at that time. Re-forecasting requires the executives to challenge those assumptions every month and ask whether those assumptions are still valid or whether they need adjusting to re-forecast going forward for the rest of the year.

Wright

So re-forecasting has to do with updating the original budget every month based on the new plan?

Christie

Yes. When we create a budget at the beginning of the year, that budget is outdated the minute that we finalize it. There are two distinct principles here—the budget and the budgeting process. Re-forecasting is a part of that budgeting process, and each month when we review the actual versus budget, we are able to see the variance.

Many companies will stop there having identified their gap. Taking it to the next level is the re-forecast. This requires an analysis of what is likely to happen based on everything you know today, not as it was assumed when the full twelve-month fiscal budget was put together prior to the start of the fiscal year. We get smarter and smarter as each month of the year goes by, so for every month that goes by, we plug in the actual numbers for the most recent month. This allows us to know a little more about what is really happening than what we knew at the end of the prior month. We know more about the external circumstances, like the economy and the competition. We know a little bit more about our own internal systems, and processes, and team members.

V-CAAR is a process about taking the best of the best information every month and then forecasting forward, based on new assumptions that reflect up-to-date knowledge to better re-forecast assumptions for the remainder of the fiscal year.

Wright

So what is your definition of a strategic plan?

Christie

Strategic planning should be the most important leadership accountability in the job description of a CEO. It's a higher level, big picture thinking looking out no more than three to five years in today's rapidly changing economy. It includes asking questions like, what business are we in, what are our products and services, what markets are we serving, and who are our potential key customers?

Wright

So how do the operational plan and budget fit in?

Christie

The Strategic Streamlining ideally is the first stage of this process. Every company should have a strong vision that is shared with everybody within the organization. The operational piece is breaking it down to who does what and by when. I'm a big fan of simplicity, "keep it specifically simple" (the KISS principle) and you're a lot more likely to do it. For example, pose the question to your management team: "What are the top three to five operational objectives that will bring us closer to our strategic vision?" Typically, the operational planning process spans the fiscal year and is further broken down into ninety-day increments for a higher level of operational focus.

The budget should be created based on the activities defined in the operational plan. Many companies will use the budget as a plan in itself, which is certainly one way of doing it, but probably not the most effective way. The process of creating a written operational plan requires a certain kind of thinking from many team members and also creates a documented path for accountability.

Wright

I'm really interested in V-CAAR as a system. Would you tell me more about V-CAAR?

Christie

Sure. The executive team would have a separate "V-CAAR" meeting one time per month, once the financials for the prior month are reported. The executive team will have prepared and submitted a report to the CEO with an executive summary of V-CAAR. The report includes a summary of the most recent month's re-forecast financial plan, the actual numbers for the prior reported accounting month, the identified variances, and a summary of the causes that have been analyzed from the prior month. Creating this report requires the executive team to hold other team members accountable by asking them to analyze the cause of the variance for the month that fits within their area of responsibility.

Now remember, variances can be either positive or negative. Variance can mean that we came in ahead of budget and this provides the opportunity to identify additional action plans to accelerate this positive result. Often times, executives will celebrate a good month without delving into the cause and can miss the opportunity to further improve their business performance.

The Action Plans, as the third step in V-CAAR, are also summarized in the V-CAAR report and the fourth step is identifying who is accountable for executing the action plans.

The Reforecast for Results is the last part of the V-CAAR report. Completing the reforecast may require meeting with all levels of employees to challenge and/or modify assumptions. This step becomes a management process and will be an important tool in providing staff motivation. The level of communication improves with staff involvement and responsibility for the future performance of the business.

Wright

So how did you create the V-CAAR?

Christie

As I mentioned earlier, the process is loosely based on the methodology from *The Executive Guide to Strategic Planning*, written by George Morrisey, Patrick Below, and Betty Acomb. We used this methodology as a solid foundation for planning. One of my mentors, Iain Macfarlane, who is also a coach within the ActionCOACH System, co-created this methodology with me as we were working with a mutual client. As we used the overall strategic and operational planning process, we recognized the need to make it more effective in today's business world and rapidly changing economy, and we accomplished this by providing an added focus on achieving results through bottom up *and* top down communications.

One of the real benefits in implementing V-CAAR beyond just improving the company's financial performance is building a stronger team. The conversations that happen as part of the strategic and operational analysis, as well as the monthly V-CAAR reporting, requires a higher level of communication than most organizations are accustomed to. The plan itself is not worth the paper it's written on—it's the thought, analysis, and conversation that go into the development of that plan that creates the real value and pulls the team together. Most importantly, this level of communication allows every level of the organization to take ownership and responsibility for the results of the plan that's been developed.

Wright

Would you tell me who should use the V-CAAR system?

Christie

This system quite frankly can be used for any size organization. Where we see the biggest affect is with the midsize companies that have multiple levels of management. The larger the organization, the more likely that departments or multiple locations may operate in silos.

The first step is to strategically designate an executive or senior management planning team. Pulling together team members from each of those departments or locations allows this planning process to become a management tool for true team-building and accountability.

Wright

So as I understand it then, if I had a midsize company and I was doing strategic and operational planning, the V-CAAR system would be something good to add in addition to that?

Christie

Absolutely. Every company that has made it to the level of being considered a midsized company must have some level of effective planning going on. When times are tough as they are right now, any holes that a company has in its operations will start to show up. I love this analogy: when times are really great it's like a big wave coming into the shore. When that wave starts to recede, what you find left on the beach is a lot of beer cans. During these difficult economic times, we are all forced to become better business owners and business leaders—and we need to take effective and streamlined planning much more seriously.

Think of the impact of having every team member, from CEO to front line staff, involved in some way in creating the top three corporate strategic initiatives. Then couple that with operational action plans for all team members that are reviewed and analyzed, at least monthly.

No matter the existing planning process the company is using, we start with what is working and then we add V-CAAR on the back end of it. V-CAAR can work with pretty much any planning process—it's about adding an extra measure of accountability and re-forecasting specific forward-looking results.

Wright

So how would an executive figure out whether this process will work with their existing planning process?

Christie

They can go to our Web site at www.ActionCoachFL.com or they can reach me by e-mail at HeatherChristie@ActionCoach.com. We have a questionnaire that we can send out to help you begin thinking about the V-CAAR process and whether it might be a good fit in your organization.

Wright

So to wrap it up here, I'm really interested in the variances in what's going on now, and if I see variances—plus or minus—then it's up to me to go to my people, analyze the cause, and then when I find the cause I set in a new action plan, or maybe an improved action plan. When I determine the accountability, then, and only then, I have the information necessary to re-forecast what the full year financial results are going to be. Am I getting it?

Christie

You're getting it; you're absolutely getting it. However, recognize that this process requires a true effort with your top executives and some powerful facilitation. Once V-CAAR has been implemented, beginning with that original strategic retreat, it's amazing to watch what happens with the team. First of all, CEOs are typically blown away because they will receive a report from their management team the likes of which they have never seen before—a simple one- or two-page report with an analysis of what happened last month and what needs to happen going forward to stay on track.

We usually do the first couple of monthly V-CAAR meetings with the client, and we find the executives involved in the process are also really excited because they've had more meaningful conversations with their team than they ever have in the past and they have an up-to-date plan in place, virtually immediately, once the prior month's financial numbers come in. It requires a whole different level of communication than usually exists in midsized companies.

Wright

So is there anything else you think I should know about V-CAAR?

Christie

Many business owners focus on profitability. In this economy, cash flow may be even more important than profitability. And V-CAAR shows the cash forecast for the company for each remaining month of the fiscal year.

The V-CAAR process takes the mystery out of financial reporting. When you focus more on the numbers, and when you do it religiously using a process that requires this kind of reporting, you create some new habits for your team members. This process transforms the way your team works together. So V-CAAR is much more than just a planning tool—at the end of the day, it is also a team-building and people development tool.

Wright

Would it be fair to say that it involves more people at different levels?

Christie

Yes. This process is truly integrated, and it's not just integrated by bringing the strategic, operations, and budget aspects together with results management. It's integrated in that it integrates the team and how team members work together.

We know that the people at the front line are often a lot more knowledgeable about operating issues than those at the top because they deal directly with our customers day in and day out. Sometimes executives are so far removed that they don't have the kind of insight that a front line employee may have. So it gives the ability for everybody—from the bottom to the top, and the top to the bottom—to have some sort of input into what is causing our results and a say in what needs to be done differently to change those results.

When an executive in a company tells me, "We're 20 percent off this year," my next question is, "So what are you going to do about it? Do you have a process in place that has you making constant improvements that will get you back on track to hit your original budget? I am assuming, of course, that the original budget was really well thought out and is important to you."

Wright

What a great conversation. I have learned a lot here today about a concept I was not acquainted with before. I really do appreciate this time you've spent with me answering all these questions.

Christie

Well, thank you. I've enjoyed having this conversation with you too, David, and I appreciate you asking me to be a contributing author.

Wright

Today we've been talking with Heather Christie, who is Co-Founder and Chairman of the ActionCOACH Business Coaching Firm in Southwest Florida. By implementing her proprietary Strategic Streamlining methodology, she brings a fresh and, as I have found out here today, a simple approach to organizations that are tired of missing their budget. This would be a good thing for me to study.

Heather, I'm so glad that you could be with us today on *Bootstrap Business.*

Christie

Thanks so much for having me.

ABOUT THE AUTHOR

Heather Christie is a Franchisor for ActionCOACH Business Coaching in the State of Florida and Co-Founder and Chairman of the ActionCOACH Business Coaching Firm in Southwest Florida. With over twenty years of business and legal experience, Heather is a professional business advisor, attorney, and professional public speaker.

As a certified Business and Executive Coach and Trainer, she was recently elected by over one thousand of her peers to receive the Global Coach's Choice Award, which is given each year to the top coach in the ActionCOACH Organization. She works primarily with midsized privately held companies to improve performance—from executive retreats to implementation of her proprietary Strategic Streamlining methodology. Heather brings a fresh and simple approach to organizations that are tired of missing their budget.

We are fortunate to have her as a contributing author for our chapter on Strategic Streamlining to share with us her expertise on her results-focused planning methodology. She has a unique background as a professional business advisor, a former partner at a prominent Chicago law firm, and a Certified Business and Executive Coach. Heather has spent the last fifteen years consulting with all levels of businesses from privately held companies to Fortune 50 executives. Her system is called V-CAAR™ and is nothing short of revolutionary for companies.

Heather Christie

ActionCOACH Business Coaching
12800 University Drive, Suite 240
Fort Myers, FL 33907
239-220-5900
www.ActionCoachFL.com
www.V-CAAR.com
heatherchristie@actioncoach.com

CHAPTER FOUR

An interview with...

Dan Kuschell

Street Smart Profit Strategies and Today's Economy

David Wright (Wright)

Today we're talking to Dan Kuschell; he is one of America's premier experts and authorities on producing massive results. You may have never heard of him, but don't let that fool you. His dream was to play pro-baseball; when that didn't work out, he got involved in direct marketing, almost 20 years ago.

Dan is one of those rare people out doing what he teaches; he spends no more than 20% of his time with training. Some of the biggest names in the world call on Dan to reveal his proven multi-million dollar ideas and strategies to generate more sales and profits. He has been behind the scenes of some of the largest marketing campaigns on and off the Internet.

Rumor has it that he has been responsible for, and part of, campaigns that have produced in excess of $30 million in business in just the last few years. He is a master of showing you how to maximize your profits and monetize your business while driving ideas deeply. At the same time, he keeps things simple for all types of people to understand.

If you're looking for practical ideas that work, Dan is truly a go-to guy for massive results. He will reveal the secrets to doubling your business, your profits, and your time off. Dan welcome to Bootstrap Business.

Dan Kuschell (Kuschell)

Well, David, I'll say it's an absolute pleasure and privilege to spend some time with you and be a part of the Bootstrap Series here.

Wright

It's obvious you're a master marketer and you've worked with several students; some who started with you were generating over $100,000 a week in less than 6 months by applying your principles. Another client is generating over $300,000 a week. Wait a minute – is that $300,000 a week? What's your secret?

Kuschell

Yeah, that's a great question and it's amazing. I've often discovered, David, that other people can say things much better than we can ourselves. It reminds me of one of the gentleman I've been fortunate to work with.

He says, "Wow, Dan. I remember when we met in a restaurant for our first meeting a few years ago. Since that time we've worked together on several projects and generated over $11 million in business together!" This from a gentleman who's one of the biggest infomercial marketers in the world today, Dean Graziosi of *Be a Real Estate Millionaire*.

You know, David, what I think it really comes down to- I'm a pretty simple person, so I guess we can dive right into it. One of the principles that I and/or my clients funnel everything we do into is called the Wealth Formula. The Wealth Formula says: "Put yourself in a position to do the work one time, and then have the ability to get paid over and over and over and over again on that work."

The second part of that principle says that you want to put yourself in a position to speak to large groups of people at a time. That's really what I've taken the time to learn and discern over the last 20 plus years that I've been in this industry. It's one of the most powerful revelations I've been able to live with and help my clients really learn with. I guess that goes to one of our main principles. We call this AIM Principle Number One.

AIM Principle Number One

If you want to have a bootstrap business and know how to truly shape an entrepreneurial business and build success, you want AIM Principle Number One. Focus your efforts in direct response marketing.

Focus your efforts in direct response marketing.

The reason being is, often times people have misconceptions about marketing or business. What I have found is that many people spend their time working *for* their business versus *on* their business. In other words, many people who start a business or run a business are really doing nothing more than buying themselves a job. That's a pretty expensive proposition right? To buy ourselves a business so we can actually have a job *in* that business.

You know, most people want the business to create lifestyle freedom and a lot of the things that money can buy. More importantly, most and all of the things money *can't* buy; freedom, peace of mind, fulfillment, joy, growth, development, challenge etc.

While I focus AIM Principle Number One at direct response marketing, we want to identify why we're in business. I find that some people have a misconception of why they're in business. There are so many reasons, but what we work with our clients to do, David, is to drive that focus, to realize that the focal point of any business should be to make a profit.

Identify why you're in business.

It's okay to make a profit. It's okay to be proud to tell people that you're in business to make a profit, because even as we look at what's going on in the economy today, we need- The country, the world, needs companies to be successful because of what it does for the GNP, what it does for the city, the community, the state, etc., in helping people with jobs and feeding the economy and so on.

So, we have to begin with the end in mind, which is not something that I invented by any means. I think it was Stephen Covey who wrote the book *7 Habits of Highly Effective People*. He says, "You have to begin with the end in mind." Our end in mind, from a bootstrap business focal point, is to work with people, to focus them on the realization that they're in business to make a profit.

Begin with the end in mind.
Realize you should be in business to make a profit.

What we find is that people fall in love with their product, so to speak. When you really look at direct marketing, what direct response marketing is to us is simply the ability to put your effort and energy into a mechanism to promote or advertise your business. This mechanism gives you an immediate response that is measurable and traceable to the bottom line, which is the profit.

If we really take the time and narrow it down and people really start to identify and put their efforts towards their direct response marketing channels, it's amazing. I often have students in our mentoring programs, David- I have hundreds and hundreds of students all over the world that I'm fortunate enough to work with; people getting started, people running multi, multi-million dollar companies.

What's amazing is that one of the common things I get is this: Dan, if you were starting all over again and you had $20,000 to start your business, how would you allocate that $20,000?

I often say, "Well, knowing what I know today, what I would do is probably take $18,000 of that and put it towards marketing. I'd take another $1,800 of it, if I were starting brand new, and I'd put it towards specialized training in that industry. Then I'd take the rest and I'd buy myself some notebooks, pens, and paperclips, and that's it. I'd go to work, build my business from cash flow, and reinvest the ideas to start small, so to speak, with your marketing channels and get the measurable response."

You know what? You're going to have some winners, but the reality in business is that you're also going to have some losers in marketing campaigns. You need to be smart enough to minimize the losers and maximize the winners. Once you find the winners, you can put more and more into growing your business and expand exponentially that campaign or group of campaigns with what we do.

You know, Michael Gerber comes to mind. I was fortunate enough to be mentored by Michael Gerber years and years ago. He's famous for the *E-myth*, and the *E-myth Revisited*, and now has a whole series of consulting programs and trainings. What's amazing is when you really know what Michael Gerber talks about in a simple sense, with the *E-myth* for example, he says, "Systems run your business", right? And finding good people to run those systems is really the key.

So, that's the idea of really working on your business. You find and develop talent that works. You work on it and grow it from a bigger perspective of time.

Find and develop talent that works, then build on it.

It ties in with the cornerstone of what we teach, David, which is the Wealth Formula: do the work one time and have the ability to get paid over and over, and put yourself in the position to speak to large groups of people at a time.

I guess I have a tendency to just go and go, and it leads me to AIM Principle Number Two in our process, which is very, very important.

AIM Principle Number Two

I've found that the hardest things for anybody to do - one of the hardest things for anybody to do at all - is to make a decision. One of my favorite books of all time, like many people in the personal growth or self-development industry, is *Think and Grow Rich*.

Chapter eight talks about the ability to make decisions. Successful people make decisions quickly, efficiently and effectively. Unsuccessful people are kind of wallowing - wishy-washy. They consider, contemplate and evaluate, and then what they frequently do is change their mind once they've made a decision. So, AIM

Principle Number Two that we really focus on as far as building a bootstrap business is make decisions based on opportunity cost.

Make decisions based on opportunity cost.

Well, you might be asking, Dan, what is "opportunity cost"? Well, opportunity cost as we define it in AIM Principle Number Two is simply this; "what's the cost of doing it", and that's a common question most people ask themselves whenever they're in a decision-making situation.

I've discovered that the other question is probably more powerful, more important and more eye opening to really find the answer, and that's "what's it going to cost you if you don't do it." Even in a bootstrap business model, applying AIM Principle One again in the marketing message is such a powerful, powerful concept to be able to work with.

Decide what the cost of doing it is, and then what the cost of not doing it is.

Why this is so important is- I guess before we get too far in it would probably be helpful if I share just a little bit about my background for everybody.

My dream, as you kind of mentioned earlier, was actually to play pro-baseball. I had what I thought was going to be a promising career taking off and then I tore a rotator cuff. Long story short I ended up coaching college baseball. I was a hitting coach, but more of a volunteer than anything.

I started looking at the industry, looking at the field, and realized, David, that if I kept working in that field I'd likely have a roommate named Dad until I was thirty-five. It didn't seem that exciting, right? Although I loved it and was passionate about it, I just didn't see it as a great vehicle that was going to allow me to build a life and a family.

So, it was around that time that I started investigating and working in direct marketing. I actually started a company in my 20's, and I did it on a handshake with a friend of mine. We got started and had some initial success, but my best friend/business partner decided he liked our bank account a little bit more than I did. He emptied it and vanished, and left me on the verge of bankruptcy.

I know there's lots of business people that have been through those kinds of things in partnerships. So I had to regroup. I did the best I could to regroup and a couple of years later I ended up being introduced to what I would say for me was the personal growth industry, the self-help industry.

I attended an event on a Friday night in Detroit, which is actually where I'm from. I grew up in the inner city of Detroit and I thought sports would be the way out, so I ended up at a Friday night overview briefing presentation, whatever you want to call it, at Cobo Hall down in Detroit.

I'll never forget it; there were a lot of happy, friendly people in this hallway and I walk in and they're talking about success, and training, and personal development and education. I have to admit that I was so excited, David, about the opportunity that was there. However, there was a catch. The catch was they said, "It's going to be $300 to attend the rest of the weekend training."

Now, I'm almost embarrassed to say this today, but I imagine there are some people that might be able to relate to this. I had spent several years working in my career and I didn't even have $300 available on a credit card or in cash resources to attend this training. So when they came to me and said, "Hey do you want to attend this training", I said, "Well, I'd love to attend the training, but I can't afford it."

I'm so thankful today, David, that I truly met a professional in that field and in that company. I can remember it was like yesterday, and I remember the gentleman I met. He said, "Well, Dan, if you can't afford it, you can't afford to pass this by."

I said, "Well, that's great and I appreciate your sales pitch, but the fact is I still can't afford it."

He said, "Well, let me ask you something-", and this is how it relates to opportunity cost, he said, "Well, Dan, what if I could guarantee you that you could increase your income to a six-figure income by what you'll learn in this two-day training? Would you find a way? Do you feel you're worth it to find a way to make that happen?"

I thought about it, and I said well yea, I think that I'd find a way. He said, "Well, Dan, I can't give you a company guarantee that that would be the case. I'll do even better; I'll give you my personal guarantee."

By the way, this leads up to AIM Principle Number Three, which is risk reversal—a very solid bootstrap business principle that we teach in our model.

AIM Principle Number Three

Risk reversal—make your offer low risk or risk free.

So long story short, what happened was that I still didn't think I had the money.

He said, "Well, Dan, how long have you been working", and I think I had been working for six or seven years up to that point of my life. He said, "Do you work pretty hard for a living", and I said, well yea. "Well, how many hours do you work?"

I said, "I don't know sixty, seventy hours a week." He said, "Well, let's just use forty since that's the average. You work fifty weeks a year-"

I said, "Well, probably more like fifty-two."

He said, "Well, that is two thousand hours a year. After five years, do you realize that's ten thousand hours that you've devoted to a system that got you to a place where you don't even have $300?"

I think it was Tony Robbins who I know has used the statement, but this gentleman used it then. He said, "Dan if you keep doing what you're doing, what you've been doing, where are you going to be next year, the year after, or five years from now?"

I said, "Well, probably the same place."

He said, "Dan, the definition of insanity-", which I believe is how Tony Robbins is defining it, "-is doing the same thing over and over again and expecting a different result. Is that what you want?" I said no. He said, "What is it going to take for you to find a way?"

What happened, David, is, this was a personal choice that I made. It wouldn't be the right choice for everybody, but it comes back to opportunity cost, and I'll come back to the principle in just a moment. My parents had sent me some money for my car payment, which was actually a couple months behind. I ended up taking some of the money they had sent me for the car and attended this event, and it was the best decision I'd ever made in my life.

I guess, officially, I became a seminar junkie at that point, because I attended, from that point on, approximately one hundred seminars over about an eight-year period. I invested about $100,000 or more in self-development, education, personal growth and training programs. For me, it became my PhD education that I never got through traditional schooling. I found it to be more valuable, I think. What I discovered from meeting, mentoring and coaching so many thousands of people all over the world, David, is that it's probably been the best education money could buy, especially when you look at opportunity costs.

So I ended up attending that event, David. I got involved in an organization applying the direct marketing principles. I actually struggled for about five or six years in that organization, but I just loved what I did. I was learning new skills, learning new talents, and I'd go to these trainings and then come back and apply it on Monday and the next couple of weeks. Then I'd go to another training and it was like this constant evolution going on.

Finally, after a handful of years, I was still struggling. Quite frankly, I often kid that after about seven years with that particular direct marketing company I was about $1.2 million away from being a millionaire. So I was frustrated quite honestly, and what ended up happening is I was ready to leave the industry. I thought Dan Kuschell was destined to just be average. I thought being in business for myself was for someone else. I was reevaluating my existence at that point.

I remember I ended up driving from where I was in Nashville, Tennessee to Louisville, Kentucky to meet one of my mentors, Laurie. I was going to let her know that I was probably going to leave the industry. I was still hand-to-mouth after so many years, and I still didn't feel like I was that much further ahead than the day I got started. I'll never forget, David, because Laurie shared something with me. I realized that, up until that point, I was really good at talking the talk, versus walking the talk.

AIM Principle Number Four

Lead by example and grow rich.

This leads to AIM Principle Number Four here, which would be lead and grow rich, and that's simply leading by example. What ended up happening when I revealed this to her was, she said, "Dan, you know what I was going to ask you. I've heard some amazing things about you, and I believe if you and I worked together we could break every record in the industry and in the company." I was like, who is she talking about?

What I realized is that my self-image, David, which is so important in business and personal success, my self-image, was that of mediocrity and probably less. I didn't see myself true. Yeah, I was good at talking the talk and telling people about principles and concepts and so on, but as far as walking the walk and truly living as that person, I just wasn't doing it.

She took me to another level in that moment. You've interviewed countless hundreds, if not thousands of people with Insight Publishing and inspire so many people in the work that you do. The fact of the matter is, David, for me my self-image was so small. I was hearing Laurie in that moment - it was a defining moment - and that defining moment suddenly got me to open up. In her eyes, she saw me as somebody, and therefore now in my eyes *I* saw me as somebody.

That's one of the powerful things that we do in our program and now it's evolved in our program. We call this the basis of our Prosperity Formula. She said, "Why don't you come work with me in Florida", and quite frankly, David, financially I wasn't ready--talk about bootstrap business, I was behind bootstrap, I was operating a 'shoelace' business.

What ended up happening was, she proposed a question, "Come work with me", and financially I wasn't really in a good position. I had a few hours to drive back from Louisville to Nashville and really consider the proposition, and I had that little voice that we get.

I actually had two voices. One voice was going, "What if this works, this is amazing, oh my gosh this in incredible, you're going to be able to do the things you've always wanted." The other little voice was going, "What if it doesn't work", and the first voice was responding, "what if it does", and the other little voice was saying, "oh my God this is an opportunity of a lifetime", the other voice, "you can do it." The other voice, "You've spent seven years; you're horrible at this."

Finally, I went back and I made a personal commitment, which I believe is another powerful concept for people; you have to make a personal commitment. What do I mean by commitment? I think the easiest way I can describe it is an analogy.

When someone walks up to the alter on their wedding day to get married, and they go up to the minister or whoever is marrying them and doing the vows, we usually say something along the lines of "'til death do us part." We don't say, "'til death do we part" with an asterisk meaning "okay, I'll be faithful twenty-nine days out of the month, but that one day a month is mine." To me, I see people in business where their commitment is one of the asterisk models versus one of the "I'm committed thirty days of every thirty days of every month", which isn't always easy. So I made a personal commitment and said, "Laurie, I'm going to do it. I'm going to be there."

What ended up happening is I had to really make a choice, because up to that point I realized I had been talking the talk, but not walking the walk. I know people all the time who say, what was it you did that changed it? So today, it's the basis of what we refer to as the Prosperity Formula. There's a whole lot more to it, but I'd like to reveal three key parts of the Prosperity Formula in just a minute.

Prosperity Formula

I came up with a journal concept, and I didn't invent it I had attended hundreds of seminars up to this point, and taken all this material and then condensed it down to something that I could easily apply myself. I'm a pretty lazy person actually, and it needs to be pretty simple to do.

So first of all, I identified the self-concept of who I needed to be as a leader. What I did was figure out the characteristics that I need to live as, Dan Kuschell at his fullest potential, and I wrote down those characteristics and qualities. The next thing I did was force myself to answer three key questions on a daily basis in the morning and then at night. It took no longer than ten minutes in the morning and ten minutes at night, but these three questions changed the direction of my future.

Now, because we've shared this with hundreds of thousands through our radios shows, TV shows, the information products, the book seminars and programs that I've been able to share with people, we have changed countless of hundreds of thousands of people's lives. I truly hope that people will take these questions, apply them and test them for the next two to three weeks. See what it does for them, see how it opens up their spirit, heart, and mind to attract truly what they desire, mentally, physically, socially, spiritually, as well as financially, in what we refer to as a holistic success approach, personally and professionally in business.

So the first question is what am I grateful for now? What am I grateful for *right now*? The second question is; what am I happy about *right now*? And the third question is; what have I done well today?

What am I grateful for right now?
What am I happy about right now?
What have I done well today?

The first time I sat down and decided to do this process before I went to work with her directly, was when I came back from this meeting in Louisville, Kentucky. The first time I wrote the question. What am I grateful for, I have to admit I was at point in my life where I wrote down one thing and then sat there and stared at my notebook for what seemed like hours. It was probably a few minutes, but it seemed very heavy in the moment, if you know what I mean.

David, really what it comes down to with the Prosperity Formula, is we look at what am I grateful for right now, what am I happy about right now and then what have I done well today. You know, one of the things I've discovered is there's a process of manifestation that happens. The more we find to be grateful for, the more we identify what we're happy about, the more that we will be happy about. The more we identify what we are doing well, the more we will have to do well.

There's a philosophy by Mark Victor Hansen who says, "You've got to be, to do, to have", and the beauty of that is what I've discovered today. The basis of the Prosperity Formula really channels people automatically. I don't know how the lights turn on when I flip a switch, David, but I just know that when I touch the switch the lights do come on. I've learned that the Prosperity Formula does that for people personally and professionally as far as how it works to build a bootstrap business.

Wright

So, there's a lot of so-called Internet guru's out there today, what makes you so unique?

Kuschell

That's a great question. I think that one of the biggest things, David, which makes me unique, is the fact that I'm actually doing what I teach. I can't tell you how many people that I've met that are out on the platform and teaching in the self help circles that are teaching concepts they used to apply, but may not be applying currently. So what I do David, is I make a focused effort, but I spend literally 80% of my time doing the things that I teach and only roughly 20% of the time teaching.

One of the beautiful things about it is it gives me the ability to learn. I've been fortunate today that on an annual basis we're doing somewhere in the neighborhood of $25 million a year, projected next year to go to another $40 million and so on for us and our clients. The beauty of that is it gives us a fun factory to play in. We can learn more in a week as far as marketing, business and real world applicable information that we're able to apply. So that would be the first thing.

The second thing is I truly get the ability to do what I love to do in this type of environment. Running a business, you know, I've had failures, which a lot of people can relate to. On the other hand I've also been fortunate over the last ten, twelve years to develop what some people consider a pretty strong level of success.

AIM Principle Number Five

That gets me to AIM Principle Number Five here, which is very important. Regardless whether someone works with me or our organization I would recommend applying AIM Principle Number Five, which is modeling success; find somebody who has the results that you want, do what they do, and you can get what they've got.

Find someone who has the business model with results you want, and do what they do.

I think that as far as the core- really, where the rubber meets the road, David, I would have to say that without a doubt that's one of the biggest things that makes me unique and us unique in our training methodologies. We're actually doing these things.

Wright

Of all the stuff we've been talking about here, today in the mentoring program you offer students and subscribers - and I know you'll be talking more about the Internet - but what about the people listening who are not technology geeks? What about those who are reading this book and listening to this CD? Are they going to be able to know what you are talking about?

Kuschell

That's also a great question. I know sometimes when we meet people we start throwing around terms related to the Internet, and they think that I must be some kind of Internet or programming expert. Admittedly, David, just a handful of months ago I finally figured out how to get Outlook on my computer, and that was only because one of my IT people got tired of me complaining about my email account. I have a staff of over 160, 170 people in my companies and they said, "Well, let me just hook it up for you." I didn't even know how to hook up Outlook in my computer, so that should probably tell somebody what my level of technical capabilities on the Internet is.

What I do is, I'm a very conceptual person, and I access resources. That's another principle that we recommend, to find the thing that you are good at, do the most productive thing at every given moment. For me the most productive thing is not to worry about writing HTML code, or doing FTP or programming, again because of the previous mentoring I've been blessed to have.

I met a mentor who says, "Spend your time focusing on the marketing aspect of your business," and so that's what I do, then I work to delegate the other stuff. So for someone who is not technical, David, the beauty is I keep it simple. I think that would be another thing that makes me unique, because I can take very complex ideas and concepts and really simplify them for just about anybody who is serious and excited to learn, an easy way to understand.

Wright

So how about somebody that's brand spanking new? Can they take advantage of your program?

AIM Principle Number Six

Kuschell

Absolutely. Often it comes back to creating systems and AIM Principle Number Six.

Use systems to run your business and good people to run your systems.

People talk about the Internet, and I've kind of been behind the scenes, David. I'm not out in the front. I'm not that active as far as promoting what we really do; there are many people who meet me and don't even know I run the companies or have the staff that I do, and that's by my own personal choice. I'm actually a very private person. As far as someone getting started brand new; let's call this system number one, the Online Internet Model, for our time and energy is one of the fastest, easiest, and low risk ways for anybody, virtually anybody, large or small to get started.

The Online Internet Model

So I'll give this step number one, which number one we would say research the market place. So many people fall in love with their product concept, and what we believe is you want to fall in love with the market. In other words, don't reinvent the wheel to try to create an entire new market place, rather find a market of hungry fish and go fish there.

One of my dear friends and colleagues, Joshua Shafran, he's the publisher of Net Profits on Demand and netprofitsondemand.com. You want to find the *'aholics'* in a market. It's more important to find the *aholics* in a market, people who truly want it, and buy it, and want more of it over and over again. This is more important than trying to reinvent the wheel, then once you do, once you find a hungry market for what you're offering, it's easy to create what we refer to as a market to message match. So step one would be research the market.

Step Number One: Research the market place.

Step two in getting started would be creating a lead opt-in page. Now there are a lot of terms out there on the Internet that people use, people call this a squeeze page, and people call it a lead capture page, and a web page, all it is simply is a page designed to one main thing, and that's to generate a lead. The most important, important, important, aspect that any business owner can have, especially somebody that is running a bootstrap business, that's the most important asset they have, is their database.

Step Number Two: Create a lead opt-in page.

So we focus in working with people to train and educate them on how to be able to build a lead opt-in page process. Very simply someone can go to, for example, our website and prosperitybasedliving.com and see a great example and model that page, or they could go to one of our colleagues, Tellman Knudson. Go to Listcrusade.com and get an example of a good lead opt-in page. Now it's not a fancy website, it's a very simple one-page introduction to invite someone to get more information, nothing more, nothing less.

If someone isn't interested in getting that introduction, that introductory information, they're not going to be learning about products that you're selling, or services that you're selling or about you or about anybody, about anything you offer if they're not interested in that first. So we believe that step two is building the lead opt-in page sequence.

Step Number Three: Add a thank you page offer.

Step three, as part of that sequence would be a thank you page offer. See, there are two distinct pieces of the model in system one, David, and that would be identifying what is it you're doing, what is the outcome you want.

Initially we believe that the most powerful thing somebody can do number one upfront is build their database, or list, and number two, then make a sale. Where we see a lot of marketers go wrong, or a lot of business owners go wrong on the Internet, trying to do both at the same time.

However, when you separate the two functions, when you focus your efforts just on the one thing of building lists, or the one thing of making a sale through the process, there is no limit and you increase your results exponentially. So the thank you offer is a good example. Again, the easiest way for someone to get an example of this is to go to our website at prosperitybasedliving.com, put in their name and email address, and it will take you to an example of a thank you page offer to model. Basically, it says thank you for subscribing, please put this email address on your safe list.

Step two says, "Discover the secrets here, and here's a homework assignment, and it's a click here." It's a call to action to drive them to the next step, which in this case would be an offer for a product or a service.

Step Number Four: Follow up with an auto responder.

The next step, step four, would be the follow up. Now, the follow up happens in the online environment through an auto responder sequence. So there are auto responders you can go to - you can go to MyARsystem.com - and it's a great toolkit that someone can set up in a matter of minutes. Basically it's a third party list management program. It's one of the best: online list management as well as deliverability, which are always a big issue online today.

That follow up in auto responder, by its nature, allows you to create messages. Then those messages are sent automatically. In other words, when someone comes to the page and they register and say, "Yes, I'd like to get more information or learn more about what you offer or do", it opts them in. It puts them in the auto responder, and then the responder system automatically sends a series of messages over and over again. So, that's step four.

Step Number Five: Drive traffic to the website.

Step five, David, would be traffic. Traffic to the website, and there are so many ways that you can get traffic. Now, people all the time say, "What do I do to research?" Well, I love research tools, referring back to step one, google.com, mywordtracker.com, incredible resources online, offline a great resource would be SRDS, Standard Rate and Data Service. Basically it's a published book of lists of the marketplaces that are available.

Again, research the market to drive traffic – SDRS guide, google.com, and mywordtracker.com.

Let's say there's someone who's a speaker. I know you do a lot of interviews with speakers, so let's say someone wanted to do a seminar and they were teaching personal power, for example. Well, how great would it be, David, for someone to get a list of the people who attended Tony Robbins seminars, or purchased Tony Robbins *Power Talk Monthly* subscription audio's every single month? How great would it be to have access to that information, to the people that actually bought those types of products? Well, as I'm looking in my SRDS guide right now, there are literally hundred and hundreds listed in this category to take advantage of. These people are in any type of marketplace: fishing, golfing, and just about any business that has a good market place to it.

SDRS guide has the list available for people to research, and then do many things. One, research the marketplace, but then you may want to rent the list, to send a direct mail offer to that list to offer those products or services. So those are a couple of example for getting traffic.

I could go on and on about these different types of things, the different types of traffic you could work with. People all the time ask, "Well, Dan, if you were starting brand new and wanted to get a fast start, what would you recommend?" Probably the fastest thing would be, number one, research the marketplace, and number two is to be able to use Pay Per Click and we recommend Google.

There is a line in Proverbs that says, "As a man or a woman thinks in their heart, so are they." It's not what you have in your head. Everybody knows how to lose weight: you eat less you work out more. But it doesn't mean they do it. They're going to do what's in their heart.

In your heart, you have beliefs and those beliefs make your decisions. They're going to determine how you prospect, they're going to determine how you listen or don't listen to people, they're going to determine whether you delegate or not, they're going to determine whether you write down a big goal or not, they're going to determine whether you follow through on your goals as a small business or not, whether you procrastinate or not. Whether it's through my work or someone else's, it's important for any small business owner to explore the beliefs you have in your heart and then go about changing the ones that aren't working.

Wright

Your firm specializes in large measurable change and that seems to set you apart from the host of motivational speakers. How are you different and why can your team produce large measurable change?

Klemmer

As a company, we are entirely committed to results. Most companies want to perform their exercise, lecture, or presentation and go home. We are compassionate samurai and we want to help our clients produce results. We agree to be held accountable for what we help produce.

For most of our clients, we actually guarantee results that we agree upon up front. A company called Christi Medical Clinic saved half a million dollars in two months and a million dollars in six months after working with us. If we didn't make the change, we had to return the fee that they gave us. We're the only company working with direct sales and home based businesses where we actually measure the income before somebody does a weekend seminar with us. After they complete the weekend, we publish the results to our website so that others can see the kind of results we're creating. It also creates accountability for us to do what we say we're going to do.

Wright

Can you give me an example of what you mean by core belief, or what you call sunglasses?

Klemmer

I look at beliefs like a pair of dark green sunglasses. In fact, when I speak I have a funky three-foot wide pair of sunglasses that I wear. I ask the audience to imagine that I was born with those on, that I came out of my mother's womb wearing a huge pair of green sunglasses. Now I'm 58 years old and I've had them on my whole life. I sleep with them. I golf with them. I go to work with them, go to church with them, I've never taken them off in 58 years.

If I look at a piece of paper in front of me, I'm going to say it's green because of my tinted sunglasses. Because you're wise and you care about me, you tell me that the paper is really white. You're just trying to help me out, I'm going to argue with you and suggest that you have your eyes checked. You can call me every day and tell me that the piece of paper is white and I'll never believe you. It doesn't matter how many times you say it, the paper will always appear green to me because I'm looking at it through my green sunglasses that I don't realize I'm wearing. Only if I discover that there is something called sunglasses and I go looking for them, which is one of the things we teach in our seminars, and I lift them off will I realize the truth: that the paper is really white. All the sudden I can see what I couldn't see just a second before.

That is how you produce dramatic change in an individual or a company. A company might be struggling as to how they can increase business when suddenly they have a revelation about their belief system—whether it's responsibility, abundance, or character—and all of the sudden they make a quantum leap.

Wright

Your firm does double digit millions a year, what is the biggest key you can give to small business owners?

Klemmer

As I've said, it's very important to hire people of character and then develop that character. Character is the only thing that lasts. Let's use our economic times, some people will be contribution oriented when everything is going right, but they won't be contribution oriented when times are tough. Hiring people of character makes it easy, but you must continue to develop that character to carry through dark times.

The other thing that I would emphasize is commitment. For most people, their idea of commitment is they promise they're going to do something that they only intend to do if it's convenient for them. They don't understand that a commitment means following through with your promise regardless of the circumstances. If you say you're going to do something you do it, regardless of how the economy's changed, or whatever the circumstances may be.

Wright

One of the core beliefs of a passionate samurai that you feel is important is abundance, but you have a very different definition. Can you share that with our readers?

Klemmer

There are many great definitions around abundance. I'm not saying mine's the only game in town. For example, Buckminster Fuller, who some say was a genius of the last century, would define abundance as the number of days you can exist without working and maintain your lifestyle. My idea of abundance is that your wholeness and completeness is not dependent on external circumstances.

Abundance doesn't have to involve money. In fact, this has nothing to do with money; it's a spiritual answer. If the opposite of abundance is scarcity, and scarcity is the idea that there's not enough, you can also conclude that "I'm not enough." People feel like they're not enough and try to become enough by having more money, or by getting married, or by being promiscuous, or whatever the case may be. All of those things are external and will never fill you up to the point where you feel whole and complete.

When a person sees that they're connected to whatever they want to call infinite, you're complete. For me, that infinite being is God. Only that connection can fill you up and make you feel complete, make you feel like you're enough. Once you have that, you can go into an economic time like this and feel abundant. The abundance is not based on how much money is in the stock market, the abundance isn't based no how much oil is in the ground, the abundance isn't based on how many hours in the day. If I'm connected to infinite power, there's a solution.

Wright

What then does the abundant mindset behavior look like in today's challenging times, I mean do you go out and buy a fancy car?

Klemmer

To this question, I have a yes and no answer. It depends on how a person responds. I was counseling a gentleman years ago that needed to move. He was torn between renting another $800 dollar apartment or a luxurious $1,200 apartment. Financially, he was torn as to what he should do. I said to him, "It depends on how you would respond. How do you feel about the less expensive apartment?" He said he hated it; he hated everything about it. "How do you feel about the luxury apartment?" He said he loved it. It made him feel successful and proud. He also felt that the $1200 payment would be a stretch but he could make it. I advised him to take on the slightly uncomfortable payment and choose the apartment that makes him feel good about himself. He now owns a 4.6 million apartment in New York City and that's just one of his homes. He's come a long way. Stretching himself financially motivated him to work harder to get ahead.

Someone like Robert Kiyosaki, for example, is completely different. Mr. Kiyosaki doesn't care where he lives. He'd live in a cardboard box and it's not going to affect him at all. He would move into the $800 apartment and invest the extra $400. Some people would feel burdened by the $1,200 a month payment, so a lot depends on how you respond to stimuli.

Wright

Why do you say mediocrity is the height of selfishness?

Klemmer

That is one of my favorite lines. Mediocrity really is the height of all selfishness. There are a lot of people out there that think they're not greedy because they only want enough to take care of themselves. They only work hard enough to meet their needs. At that point, you know that you're only focused on yourself.

Once you're focused on contribution, there's a bottomless pit of resources. You're going to want more money because you can serve more people, you can bless more people. If all I'm worried about is my wife, my three kids, and myself, I don't need much money to do that. But once I'm caring about the homeless out there, once I'm caring about single mothers that are trying to raise kids, once I'm concerned about all the people out there that are hurting and needing, I'm going to be motivated no matter how much money I have.

I had a network marketer named Henry that came to me and said, "I'm making $400,000 a year and I'm no longer motivated, can you help me?"

I said, "I already know the problem."

He said, "I haven't told you anything about me, how could you know the problem?"

I said, "I know all I need to know."

He said, "Well what's the problem?"

I said, "You're selfish, all you think about is yourself. All you're worried about is you and as long as $400,00 would buy a nice car, nice house, and take care of your family, you're done. That's why you're no longer motivated. But if your life was about contribution, $400,000 a year would be a drop in the bucket. You'd be motivated no matter how much money you make."

That's why mediocrity is the height of all selfishness: once you care about other people and you're contribution oriented, you're going to be motivated because you want to serve.

There are many ways to serve. I don't want people to just focus on money. After all, this is a conversation about business bootstrapping. But there are ways to be of service to children and in the community. But when people claim that they don't care about money, I think it's because they don't know how to create it. It hurts when you want to create something and can't. Allow yourself to serve people and that will create the desire for more money so that you can bless others with it.

Wright

Well Brian what a great conversation, I always learn a lot when I talk to you. It's always a pleasure and I've thoroughly enjoyed the time that you've spent answering these questions with me here today.

Klemmer

Thank you David, I hope this project is an enormous success and blesses you.

Wright

Today we've been talking to Brian Klemmer. Brian's company, Klemmer and Associates Leadership Seminars, is a character development training company specializing in producing large and measurable change in a short period of time. His latest book, *The Compassionate Samurai*, was released this year, 2008, and has been named the #1 business book for the Wall Street Journal. Brian, thank you so much for being with us today on Bootstrap Business.

Klemmer

Thank you very much David.

ABOUT THE AUTHOR

Brian Klemmer has been speaking professionally for over thirty years and has spoken in over fifteen countries. His firm, Klemmer and Associates Leadership Seminars, is a character development training company that specializes in producing large, measurable change in a short period of time. Their client list includes a dozen network-marketing companies and well-known organizations such as Aetna Health Care, Hewlett-Packard, and Suzuki Motor Company. Brian Klemmer is a West Point graduate and has shared the platform with gurus like Zig Zigler, Robert Kiyosaki, and Mark Victor Hansen. Brian's latest book, *The Compassionate Samurai,* was released in 2008 and quickly became the #1 business book for the Wall Street Journal. Brian, welcome to Bootstrap Business.

Brian Klemmer

Visit www.klemmer.com for 52 free leadership lessons

1-800-577-5447

Blog: www.bklemmer.com

CHAPTER SEVEN

An interview with...

Tom Hopkins

Networking and The Art of Selling

David Wright (Wright)

Today we're talking with Tom Hopkins. Tom is a sales legend. Many believe that natural ability is enough to make you successful in a sales career, but the truth of the matter is that natural skill combined with "how to" training is the real secret to high level productivity. Having learned this lesson the hard way, Tom is quick to admit that his early sales career was not successful. After benefiting from professional training, he became a dedicated student, internalizing and refining sales techniques that enabled him to become a sales leader in his industry.

Tom's credibility lies in his track record and the track records of the students he has trained over the years. He has personally trained over three million students on five continents. He has shared the stage with some of the great leaders of our times including Ret. General Norman Schwarzkopf, former President George Bush and Barbara Bush, Secretary of State Colin Powell, and Lady Margaret Thatcher.

Tom has authored twelve books, including *How to Master the Art of Selling* and *Selling For Dummies*™. His first book, *How to Master the Art of Selling*, has sold over 1.6 million copies and has been translated into ten languages. It is required reading for new salespeople by sales and management professionals in a wide variety of industries.

Tom was a pioneer in bringing broadcast-quality video training to the marketplace. Over 16,000 video sales training systems are utilized in-house by companies around the world. His audio cassette programs have long been lauded for their quality, comprehensiveness, along with his workbooks with word-for-word phraseology.

Through the ups and downs of a seller, a career as a business owner, professional speaker, and trainer, Tom Hopkins has maintained his dedication to the continued growth of his students. He firmly believes that everyone can benefit from utilizing his proven techniques, ideas, concepts, and values.

Tom, welcome to *Bootstrap Business.*

Tom Hopkins (Hopkins)

Well, thank you, David! And it's so nice after all these years to have a chance to visit with you.

Wright

Tom, after reading an article you wrote titled "Making Connections," it occurred to me that people coming into sales think that networking is only for high-level businesspeople. Can you explain what networking is and how new salespeople can take advantage of it?

Hopkins

First of all, when people use networking, they are taking advantage of a basic law—the Law of Reciprocity. That law basically says, "If I do something good for you, you will feel similarly obligated to do something good for me." That's what networking really is. It's getting together with groups of people who are not in your same industry—so there is no competition involved—then sharing possible leads.

For example, if you just think about it, every three years almost 95 percent of the American population will buy a new car. Every four to five years about 90 percent will buy a new home. And everyone should have help in insurance and financial services to prepare for their golden years. So if you only look at those three industries as examples, you can find people to network with.

When I first learned of this concept I decided to find the top automobile dealership salesperson, the top insurance salesperson, and I was of course in real estate. IBM had just started to blossom, so I got the number one IBM rep I could find in the area. I called them all, and found the top person in each company. We met and decided that we were going to try to find out if we could send leads to each other. And that is how my experience in "networking" began!

Today most companies ask their people to join organizations like their local Chamber of Commerce—to go wherever there's a meeting of people—and try to exchange business cards and see if they can't find a few people to build a networking opportunity with.

Many years ago it wasn't called networking, but that's what people call it today. Networking is taking advantage of what other people have to offer and they, in turn, take advantage of what you have to offer. That way you both grow to reach your goals more rapidly sending leads back and forth and having a network group.

The field of selling can beat you up—it's emotionally draining. If you have three or four people in a network you meet with who are up-lifting and can talk with you about how well they're doing and get you back on track, that's another great reason for networking!

Wright

In that same article you advocated techniques such as staying in touch, actually asking for help, and volunteering to help as methods of networking. Can you expand on these?

Hopkins

First of all, I think that's the key. I think you need to have a planning meeting in your networking group. Let's say you meet every Tuesday morning at 7:30. You meet and have a cup of coffee and you all talk about how you're doing. You then try to see if you can all bring a lead to the table that one of the folks can go ahead and contact.

Also, networking is in an excellent way a way of saying to yourself, "I'm going to try to help as many other people as I can. I'll volunteer, I might go and join as many community and charitable organizations as I can. I'm going to do my best to help, and thus I'll also network and meet all the folks in that organization."

Wright

Recently I was going through some notes I had written from another of your writings titled *Turning Little Dollars into Big Dollars*. You wrote that, "One of the biggest mistakes salespeople make is to market their product to someone and stop there." Can you explain what you mean?

Hopkins

When people invest in your product or service obviously, by making that commitment, they have said, "I like you, I trust you, and I'm happy to do business with you." But you don't stop there. I think you should send them a thank you note for doing business. You should then set up a process where you do your best to see if they might give you referrals. I've found that most people who really like and trust you at the closing of a sale will afterward be more than happy to say that they know a couple of people who might also be interested. Then you need to follow up and ask if you can help some of those folks. Many people will give you referrals.

Most salespeople make a sale and that's the end of it instead of saying, "I have a philosophy: when I sell a house, my goal is to stay in touch, follow up, and to see if I might be able to make three or four other sales over the years from referrals to people you know who are friends, relatives, and so forth."

Wright

You have said that there is an emotional process that leads to a purchase. If I remember correctly, it involves a new development in the buyer's self-image. Will you tell us what you mean and how salespeople can spot these changes?

Hopkins

I've always believed that over the years with the hundreds and hundreds of houses I've sold (my background being real estate) that I have found that the actual purchasing decision is not logical—it's *emotional*. There is an emotional thing you do with people with the right questions, by asking them certain things that create an emotional build. Too many people think that someone's going to come up with a logical reason to buy a car, a house, insurance, or whatever it is. The truth is that the final decision is made emotionally, and then buyers defend what they did logically with reasons that you as the salesperson give them.

Wright

That does sound like a process that can be learned!

Hopkins

It is. That's what's exciting—all the elements in the art of selling can be learned. And I just want to share this with all the people who might be really paying attention to this. There are two extremes of personality and temperament types: One is the interesting extrovert, and the other is the interested introvert.

The interesting extrovert is the person who's outgoing and gregarious and talkative and charming and witty. Those people gravitate into sales because they are very talkative.

On the other side of the spectrum is the interested introvert. These people are a little timid, a little shy, they don't think they can sell, they're afraid of the process of talking to strangers. The sad truth is that the interested introvert can do *better* in sales long-term than the interesting extrovert because the interested introvert is interested in other people and he or she is willing to listen. Interested introverts are great listeners, they ask questions, and they give up control of conversation. The interesting extrovert has the usual personality you'd expect of salespeople. They're talkative and overbearing, aggressive, and they want to control everything. So if you're an interested introvert, don't be afraid of selling. You can do great!

If you're an interested extrovert, just lighten up a bit and start with more questions than with trying to overtake folks by telling them what they should do.

Wright

Your students have told you that one of their biggest challenges is their clients are not loyal. What advice do you give your students to help them overcome this problem?

Hopkins

This is one thing that has changed in our culture. In fact, people sometimes ask me, "Tom, you've been doing this sales training for thirty years; what has changed?" The main thing that has changed is that people don't have the long-term loyalty with a sales representative that they used to have. There are many reasons for that. Some people who are reading this may be selling a product where the decision-maker works for a company that is just totally concerned with profit—if the decision-maker can save two cents on an item for the entire company, it could mean a lot of money, so they aren't loyal to that salesperson.

The first thing I want to say is to not be upset—that's just the way the culture is. Secondly, here are some ideas to keep clients loyal: Number One, you really have to keep in touch with them and make them realize that they will do better because of what you do. For example, if I sold computers and I had a client company with a very busy managing director or vice president who was in charge of buying computers and computer related items, if I can get some of the responsibility off him I make him look good to the whole company for what I do. As a result he will almost delegate authority to me.

I know some salespeople who don't really sell anymore. They control the company's inventory of a product. Then, of course, the decision-maker is thrilled that he or she doesn't have to worry about it. The salesperson has been given control of the inventory. He or she handles everything and is not really selling. The salesperson controls the company's inventory and earns a nice fee at the end of the year.

Wright

In my business, marketing and booking speakers, getting to speak to the right person who can make a buying decision is sometimes a difficult task. How do you suggest we get through the company "gate-keepers" and speak to the right person?

Hopkins

This is a fun little game you have to play. I hope the people reading this realize that selling or a business activity is like a game—it's a competition. Now, if I were talking to a straight sales commission person who had to market a product or service to earn his or her income, I'd say, "Hey, you have a game that you have to play to get past gate-keepers." The gate-keepers are normally those who answer the phone first, then passes the call to the executive assistant who hides the decision-maker.

Here are some of the keys, David. First, when marketers or salespeople call a company they have to come across with a different way of addressing what they are going to do. For example, I suggest they call and let's say a receptionist answers the phone. If I were doing the calling I would say, "Hi, my name is Tom Hopkins. I'm in business in the community." This creates a rapport—they're in business, I'm in business. Then I'd say, "I really need to talk to the person in your company who is in charge of increasing profits or eliminating overhead. Who might that be?"

The receptionist hears the words "increasing profits" or "eliminating overhead," and she has no idea what this means, but she's thinking this is what the company needs to do, just as all companies today need to do. That one little sentence will motivate her to get me to the decision-maker. Now often they'll say, "Well, that will be Mr. Brown, and I'll put you through to his secretary." Of course, I get Mr. Brown's secretary on the phone and I say, "Hi, my name is Tom Hopkins. I'm in business in the community and I would like to refer people to your company and show Mr. Brown ways that he might eliminate some overhead and increase profits. May I speak with him please?"

Then the secretary may stall and say, "Well, he's not available," or "He's not in," or, "Do you have an appointment?"

I reply, "Let him know I called. Would you please write this down? My name is Tom Hopkins. Make sure he knows that I'm a *local business person*, just like he is, so please, on the message would you please write 'Tom Hopkins, local business person, wanting to refer business to our company'?"

Now I'll guarantee you that when he comes in, he'll get that message and he'll ask "Who is this?"

"Well I'm not sure," the secretary will reply.

And because you didn't leave your phone number (*never* leave your phone number) he'll be curious! Here's a local businessperson who wants to refer business to the company. Remember, this is the game—it's a game you play, but when I use this method I met almost every decision-maker. Why? It was because when I called back the person will ask, "What do you mean you're going to refer business back to us?"

I'll say, "You know what? You have the largest Mercedes dealership in the city. I'm going to be working with people who want a Mercedes in the future—can I send them to your top producer?"

"Well of course!"

"Who is that?"

Now I'm building a network—the top producer now wants to meet me because I'm going to send him qualified buyers!

Wright

Tom, you are the only sales trainer I know who talks about a "No" close to clients who feel that they have to say "no." What is the "No" close?

Hopkins

David, that's funny that you'd ask because the "No" close is really an advanced close, meaning that it's not for a brand new person—it's for that person who's been out there many years in sales, and they know that there will be people right there in the beginning who have got to say "no" and you're wasting your time. The basic "No" close allows them to say "no," but the no will mean a "yes."

Let me say something and then you just say, "Tom, I just have to say no." Ready?

"David, I really feel that these financial services will be good for you and your family."

Wright

"Tom, I just have to say no."

Hopkins

"Well you know, David, there are many salespeople in the world and they all seem to have opportunities that they're confident that are good for you, and of course they have some persuasive reasons for you to invest in them, haven't they? You of course can say no to any or all of them, can't you? But you see, as a professional with my financial services, my experiences have taught me an overwhelming truth: no one can say 'no' to me. All they can say 'no' to is themselves and their company's future financial security. Tell me, David, how can I accept that kind of 'no'? In fact, if you were me, would you let me say 'no' to anything so critical to the company's future financial gain?"

Wright

That is great.

Hopkins

And you'd say, "No, no I wouldn't," which is why it's a "No" closer. I'm the only one who teaches that. I'm also telling the people, "Listen, Ace, they recorded that. You really have to know what you're doing and be a pro. Ace, you have to have the guts to try it." In fact, that's the truth of all closing skills—you have to have the guts to continue with the attitude, "What do I have to lose? Let's try one more word, one more phrase, and maybe I can take a 'no' into a yes!"

Wright

You have said that your years of experience with millions of salespeople have proven to you that the top people have one important characteristic in common: they are good listeners. Most people think salespeople have the "gift of gab." Would you explain the difference?

Hopkins

Most salespeople do have a gift of gab. In a way they are talkative and communicative; but they need to learn the discipline of shutting up and asking questions. If you're the opposite of what the buyer expects—meaning I'm not a big talker, I'm a better listener—I'll start off my presentation by having in essence four or five questions.

For example, I might say, "David, before I talk to you about advertising with our radio station, it's not fair for me to tell you what we can do until I find out if you really have a need for our service because I don't want to waste your time. Can I ask you a couple questions? Who are you using now for your advertising?" I'll find out what your past experiences are with my questions and then I'll find out what you enjoyed about what you've been doing with these companies. Then I'll find out what changes you'd like to make, and eventually I'll open your mind up with questions. The prospect might then ask me, "Why don't you write up what you can do for us to see if we might want to consider it?" That's the whole key—get that little door open and I'll open the whole company for my business.

Wright

In an article about listening, you advocate questioning and encouraging others. Instead of being pushy, you suggest a salesman be "pulling." What do you mean by "pulling"?

Hopkins

Pushy means I make a statement like, "David, we are the best! You should do business with us!" That's a statement. A question is, "David, we spent years developing our rapport with customers and clients like you, and you agree with me that if we're professional and can help you, then it might make sense to look into what we can do for you." You see the difference? The statement: "We're the best, you need what we can do, you should buy this," is a sentence that contains all statements. The pro thinks about, "How can I make it a question?"

Here's another example of pulling: "Now I just want to ask you this, David: I know you're probably very financially well off, but if I can show you how to retire eight years sooner with ten times more money than you have right now, would you at least listen to what I have to say?"

Wright

That does make sense!

Hopkins

It does! And that's a great sentence, by the way. To you guys and gals in sales: everything must not only make sense, but it must trigger your prospects' desire to know more and be curious about what you can do for them.

Wright

The first time I met you we talked about real estate. I was running a real estate company in Tennessee and you had a great selling program. Five years after that my company was closing eleven hundred single-family dwellings. Today that would be about 150 million dollars. Your record of helping people grow is outstanding.

Who taught you the principles you now teach and helped you get to where you are today?

Hopkins

The very first person was my mother. My mother was a wonderful woman who treated people so beautifully. She would come home after going out to dinner with a couple and she'd sit down and write a thank you note. That's where I first learned about thank notes—from my mom! She also had a wonderful attitude of gratitude—she was very thankful, she thanked God for her blessings. She was a very spiritual woman and she passed that on to me.

Then of course I met people who were top producers. They were not interested in the money as much as making people happy and making clients happy. There's nothing greater than selling a product, making a fee and income, and then having them thank you for doing it for them! That's when you really are great.

Wright

So what do you see on the horizon for those who would choose sales as a career? Will sales always be a rewarding and exciting career for people just starting out in business?

Hopkins

I believe that selling is the lowest paid "easy" work, and the highest paid "hard" work in the world.

New people in sales have to put a commitment of two or three years of building their business until it's all referrals, but there's nothing better than being in business for yourself! And I will say this: the average American wants to own their own business and wants to be in charge of their destiny, but most people don't have the ability or the money to open up a big company because they don't have the cash to say, "Here's $150,000."

You can find a company with a great product that you really believe in. That's the key—you must love the product, you must believe in the product. The reason I did so well in real estate is I totally believed that real estate is the foundation of this entire country's financial base, and the folks who own more real estate will have more net worth and so forth. You've got to believe in what you sell.

To all of our readers: find a product you love and believe in; give up a paycheck and learn the profession of selling! I can teach you every word to say, and then you'll be amazed at how much money you can make.

Wright

Lastly, what is in the future for Tom Hopkins? Where do you go from here after all your successes?

Hopkins

I'm asked that often. Many people have been with me in my training sessions for twenty-five to thirty years. They say, "Hey, you don't have to leave Scottsdale, Arizona, and do a seminar! Why do you still go out and do it?" I've got to say this (and I hope people grab this): if you have a talent to do something that helps your fellow man, and God's blessed you with that, I believe that you have an obligation to do it!

To retire at my age and sit back and play golf every day, although I could, I don't believe that's what I should do. I think I spent twenty-five to thirty years building a reputation. Now, when I come into most cities all the seminars are selling out because people say, "Hopkins teaches the truth and what really works in closing sales!" So I really believe that my future is to train more people than any other person.

Let me give you an example, David. There's been no human being who has done 5,000 seminars in his or her career. I'm at 4,576 right now. My goal before I die is to say, "I did 5,000 seminars!" Then I'll feel that my legacy and my talents have been used. All those people I've touched have had the chance to have better lives, more income, and more growth. If I've done that, I think I have achieved what I'm supposed to achieve as a human being.

Wright

You don't mind if I go home and tell my wife that you said it's okay for me to keep working?

Hopkins

Yes, yes—let her know that we are both going to keep working!

Wright

Absolutely—this is what I'm supposed to be doing!

Hopkins

That's right! David, just remember that "working" is something you're doing when you'd rather do something else. My life has *never* been work. When I was in real estate it wasn't "work," I loved it! When I get up on the stage and do my seminars, I'm not "working"—I am helping people financially grow. So if you're still "working," find something you love to do where the money isn't important—something you just *love* to do and do it!

Wright

What a great conversation. I always enjoy talking with you. I always go away from our conversations thinking I can do anything in the world.

Hopkins

Well, thank you, David. I enjoyed talking with you again. All the best to those reading this!

Wright

We've been talking today with Tom Hopkins who is a sales legend. His credibility with me lies in his track record. He's proud of that track record—he has trained over 3,000,000 students on five continents, and he has shared the stage with some of the great, great speakers and leaders of our time.

Tom, thank so much for being with us today on *Bootstrap Business.*

ABOUT THE AUTHOR

Tom Hopkins is a sales legend. Many believe that natural ability is enough to make you successful in a sales career, but the truth of the matter is that natural skill combined with "how to" training is the real secret to high level productivity. Having learned this lesson the hard way, Tom is quick to admit that his early sales career was not successful. After benefiting from professional training, he became a dedicated student, internalizing and refining sales techniques that enabled him to become a sales leader in his industry.

Tom's credibility lies in his track record and the track records of the students he has trained over the years. He has personally trained over three million students on five continents. He has shared the stage with some of the great leaders of our times including Ret. General Norman Schwarzkopf, former President George Bush and Barbara Bush, Secretary of State Colin Powell, and Lady Margaret Thatcher.

Tom has authored twelve books, including *How to Master the Art of Selling* and *Selling For Dummies*™. His first book, *How to Master the Art of Selling*, has sold over 1.6 million copies and has been translated into ten languages. It is required reading for new salespeople by sales and management professionals in a wide variety of industries.

Tom Hopkins

www.tomhopkins.com

CHAPTER EIGHT

An interview with...

Brenda Hill-Riggins

Success in a Recession

David Wright (Wright)

Today we are talking with Brenda L. Hill-Riggins. She is the president of Mars Contractors Inc., a successful family owned and operated construction company. Steered by mother wit and tenacity and as the surrogate visionary, Brenda, with her husband, Marcus, has brought the company a long way in a short period of time. Mars Contractors is committed to insuring complete client satisfaction in the area of HVAC, plumbing, and general contracting by delivering quality services through an innovative blend of technology and management expertise.

With a strong desire to fulfill her purpose, which is to help others understand their purpose and move her coaching clients more quickly to their desired destinations in life, in 2007, Brenda transitioned from what she does (a contractor) to who she is—an author, speaker, and life coach. She still oversees and manages the company. She completed her speaker's training at The Motivational Center with Dr. Tina Dupree. Brenda completed her coaching training at Florida International University. Brenda received her life coach certification from and was personally trained by Dr. Martha Beck, Oprah Winfrey's life coach expert, *New York Times* bestselling author, and *O Magazine* monthly contributor. As the beloved originator of the Royal Collection, a line of inspirational products she manufactured, Brenda L. Hill-Riggins fostered the emergence of an understanding from an individual perspective and has plans to watch it grow to a billion-dollar market.

Brenda, welcome to *Bootstrap Business*.

Brenda L. Hill-Riggins (Hill-Riggins)

Thank you. Thank you for having me.

Wright

Why did you and Marcus start the business?

Hill-Riggins

When I first met Marcus, it was his dream to own his own company. He was working as a plumber and was a member of a local trade organization. I told him that I could help him if he was willing to trust me. Marcus concentrated on securing his state license, which is needed in order to do business the right way. I began setting up the business while he finished his studies for the state license and took the test. The test results came back three days before Hurricane Andrew hit. Hurricane Andrew was ranked the most costly and one of the most devastating storms in U.S. history; that was in 1992. It tore up South Florida really bad. After waking up that morning and seeing the total devastation in the area we felt empty, but after a day or two, we began to see the silver lining in the mist of the devastation. We thought about things and said, "Oh my God! Look at the business opportunity!" Needless to say, we were able to launch the business.

In the next several months, we actually secured over a million dollars in business. Business was not easy. We were faced with not being able to secure loans for working capital,—payroll, purchase material, etc. We focused on doing one or two jobs at a time. Performance was the key. We had to grow the company based on our own initiative, resources, and abilities without relying on outside help.

Wright

What do you think a business needs most?

Hill-Riggins

Now this is sixteen years later and hindsight is 20/20, but I think what a business owner needs most before starting a business is an understanding of the industry that he or she plans to operate in. Why is this the key? An understanding of the industry will allow the business owner to know what resources are available, how to go about gaining access to those resources, and who the key players are.

For example, political alliances can be an asset to the growth of your business. Know what the plans are for the segment of the industry you wish to enter, and network with the leader who can develop and approve those plans.

Wright

What is the definition of "entrepreneur" to you?

Hill-Riggins

To me, an entrepreneur is a self-reliant individual who has the ability to make good decisions on the spot using an accelerated thought process while assuming the risk of the endeavor he or she undertakes. I also think that entrepreneurs are people who are created for business. It's a gift to provide good service. Once they understand who they are—entrepreneurs—they are able to connect to that special ability that is within them. They will activate forces that will alleviate the disconnects that hinder success.

Wright

What do you think makes a great entrepreneur?

Hill-Riggins

One who has great insight, foresight, and hindsight.

Wright

What are the core values of the company's culture?

Hill-Riggins

First of all, we to try to make sure that we do things in a godly fashion in all areas of life and in business—to operate with values and morals, integrity and fairness. We always strive to live by the Ten Commandments, as well as allow our actions to be governed by the golden rule at all times, making sure that ethics is first and foremost in our business practice. We try to make sure we approach our daily task as a team with the understanding that it is not all about us. We have been given a great responsibility as business owners and as employers to pull ourselves up by our own "bootstrap," and teach others and employees to be self-initiating and self-sustaining.

Wright

Probably most people would think that construction is a man's world. Why did you choose to work in a male dominated industry?

Hill-Riggins

I was raised in construction. My father was a small contractor. I guess that after my oldest brother left home, I was next in line to assist him. I became very familiar and comfortable in this male dominated environment. I have not had any major problems as a female. I did not choose the industry, the industry chose me. In honor of the late Elijah Hill, I will always be a builder.

In construction, the goal is to have a solid foundation, a strong infrastructure, straight walls, and a roof with great supports. I apply these same concepts to life.

Wright

Let's talk about business plans for a minute. What do you think is a good business plan?

Hill-Riggins

I believe that a good business plan is one that is based upon the vision of the person who actually operates the business. It also takes into account the short earnings of this individual and implement steps to overcome these obstacles. Additionally, a good business extends to having a development plan. Of course, when I started everyone said you've got to have a good business plan and of course I went through the process and created one. What I have learned over the years is that it is good to create a development plan for your life inclusive of your family before doing a business plan as well so that your family and business grow together. A development plan is a personal plan centered on your total vision for your life. And not just what you plan to do, but perhaps what God has commissioned you to do. It is more from a godly perspective and more in sync with your purpose as opposed to just a career or a particular type of business you would like to have. It is not about making money but fulfilling a need.

Wright

What was your strategy for securing contracts?

Hill-Riggins

Once we joined a couple of trade organizations, we found out real fast that there were a lot of opportunities that are in sync with the small business participation goals on a lot of projects, especially government, local, county, or federal contracts. Business is hard; competition can be tough. We made the decision to focus on these types of contracts to help jump-start the business. We work hard to be able to present MARS Contractors, Inc. as a contractor of choice for Prime Contractors. We went after projects that afforded us an opportunity based on small business participation goals, and it worked.

Wright

Can you explain your strategic plan?

Hill-Riggins

In the beginning the plan was very simple. Own our business, work our business, and mind our own business. As time and life began to test us, the goal for success became success without struggle. Our focus was on technology, implementing the right systems and processes, and understanding the method behind our own madness. To secure sales we made sure MARS Contractors, Inc. was in the data bases of the different state, local, or federal agencies so that prime contractors would know where to find us. Then we tried to make sure that as we grew in sales, that we strengthened our foundation, which included adding to the team.

Our strategy included securing high profile projects to help sell the company's ability to perform on bigger and more complex projects. We went after projects like the American Airlines Arena and Tampa Bay Stadium; both were high profile jobs that brought us high profile visibility.

On this new level we met new "devils." We did not run from these new challenges but instead took time to learn the lessons that would give us the right to move forward in the future. Nothing happens in construction until after the political process. We participated in the political process but in a good ethical way, of course. Our strategy was to position ourselves so that we could participate as a capable small business or minority company on the larger projects and it worked well for us.

We've just won the construction management contract with two other larger companies to build the $500 million Marlins Baseball Park here in Miami.

Wright

What do you think about today's economy?

Hill-Riggins

I really get frustrated when I hear larger companies—insurance companies and banks—asking to be bailed out, especially the banks. We were never fortunate enough to secure any loans from the banks. I learned banks loaned money to people who really didn't need it. What is the real purpose behind banking anyway? I feel they are failing because they have failed the community.

Now that they are hurting, they want the government to bail them out. I don't think it should happen. I think that if they do not have the ability to manage money, they really do not need to be in the business where money is the commodity. Their Beacon score must be below 100.

Their leaders did not do the projections necessary to identify disconnects within the profit and loss statements they require business owners in general to understand and know. They get an F!

I also feel that greater focus should be put on small banks that are in the black and performing well and give them the support and an opportunity to grow. Allow the smaller well-performing banks to mentor the larger failing banks. I don't think that anybody should be bailed out. The emerging bankers are in a different mindset, they are greater thinkers and process information differently based on technology. They are more in sync with the new times and can move the banking industry forward.

Wright

Does your organization perceive itself to be dominant, submissive, harmonizing, or searching out a niche?

Hill-Riggins

We are searching for a niche while trying to maintain harmony in the industry. We have hopes to be dominant in the future. I feel that we will be a force to reckon with very soon because we have done things the right way. We have planted the right seeds—we are experiencing success in a recession. In the past we have been in survival mode and sometimes on life support, but not today. In hopes of being dominant someday, we will continue to strive to keep things in perfect harmony.

Wright

What local agencies—government or federal agencies—have assisted you or have been most helpful in procuring contracting opportunities?

Hill-Riggins

Miami Dade County has done an absolutely wonderful job assisting small businesses. I moved here eighteen years ago. After attending a few of their workshops and consulting with the director at the time, Gregg Owens, I thought to myself, "What opportunity!" If you ever have a desire to own your own business and conduct business the right way, this was the place.

The Business Development Department has many resources in place to assist entrepreneurs. I felt that we could write our own ticket no matter what business we decided to create. I think that Miami Dade County has done just an outstanding job in helping small businesses. MARS Contractors, Inc. has been able to experience success on many different levels. Also, the Department of Defense has really worked well with us.

The private company that has provided MARS Contractors, Inc. the greatest opportunity in the life of the company is the Hunt Construction Group. I have found them to be truly committed to diversity and the community.

Wright

Do you feel the existence of a glass ceiling?

Hill-Riggins

Yes. There is a glass ceiling with different elements that gives it its strength. Concentrating on trying to shatter it can take you away from your goals. There is a way to break those glass ceilings and keep focused on your business at the same time, but you must be very strategic with what you do and how you do it.

I feel that we have broken glass ceilings. We stayed focused by performing and doing the right thing, making sure that our company is strong, and being viable in our community and within our families. One of the ways we broke the ceiling was by accepting the challenges brought on by those who created the glass ceilings—

playing their games while in possession of the rule book. There is a message you send out just by doing the right thing that allows you to surpass what most people can't do. It is important to remember that it is not all about you or your company. When you do good, goodness has to come back to you; and if there is any type of ceiling between you and goodness, that ceiling (negative energy) will self destruct.

Wright

What are your most significant company achievements?

Hill-Riggins

MARS Contractors, Inc. is sixteen years old. The most significant achievement is knowing we are experiencing the success we envisioned. We pulled ourselves up by our own bootstrap. We took advantage of the resources made available through the efforts of community leaders to ensure small business participation on contract opportunity.

In a time of a recession, our company is stronger than it has ever been. Peace is the greatest gift and gratitude is the greatest feeling. I know that a lot of our counterparts are struggling and a lot of business owners have not been able to maintain. But after all that we have been through, we are still here and we are stronger than ever.

At the end of the day, everybody is paid and everybody is good and our future is really bright with a lot of great opportunities. In the words of Oprah Winfrey, "My future looks so bright, it burns my eyes."

Wright

How does the company measure success?

Hill-Riggins

We measure success by being able to help and give without hesitation or regret. Recently we gave our employees paychecks early because of the Thanksgiving holiday. I heard one of them say, "Good. I've got my mortgage to pay." Being able to provide jobs with a good pay is success. Being able to help others throughout the year is success. Being able to send our children to college, eliminating worry about having to get grants and loans—that's success. We have been able to help a lot of others in the family to move forward—that's also success. When the local football team comes to us and we are able to give a check, that too is success. There are so many ways that we can measure success, but it is the little things that we are able to do for our employees, ourselves, our families, and the community (i.e., when we are able to give) that makes us successful.

Wright

Well, what a great conversation. I really learned a lot. As an entrepreneur I can really respect what you have done in the last several years. My hat's off to you. I know that our readers are really going to learn a lot by reading this chapter.

Hill-Riggins

Thank you.

Wright

Today we have been talking with Brenda L. Hill-Riggins who is president of Mars Contractors. She has a strong desire to help others understand their purpose and to move her coaching clients more quickly to their desired destinations. In 2007, she transitioned from what she does as a contractor, to who she is—a transformation coach. She is affectionately known as "The Transformation Coach." Brenda fostered the emergence of an inspirational understanding from an individual perspective and she plans to watch it grow to a billion-dollar market. She is the mother of four and grandmother of eight, a world traveler, loves to cook and entertain, and is learning to be a farmer. She resides in beautiful Miami, Florida, with her husband, Marcus, and their dogs Bear and Focus.

Brenda, thank you so much for being with us today on *Bootstrap Business*.

Hill-Riggins

Thank you so much for having me and God bless you.

ABOUT THE AUTHOR

Brenda L. Hill-Riggins is President of MARS Contractors, Inc., a successful family owned and operated construction company. Steered by mother wit and tenacity, Brenda and the team has brought the company a long way in a short period of time. MARS Contractors, Inc. assists with the process, quality, and transference of forces producing and controlling the physical world and its phenomena with the movement of air and water—the essentials for life. MARS Contractors is deeply committed to the best interest of their clients, as well as humanity as a whole. MARS Contractors, Inc. is committed to ensuring complete client satisfaction by delivering quality services through an innovative blend of technology and management expertise.

With a strong desire to help others understand their purpose and move her coaching clients more quickly to their desired destinations in life, in 2007, as an individual, Brenda transitioned from what she does (a contractor) to who she is—a transformation coach. Brenda has given the vision of the company back to her husband, Marcus, to carry. Brenda still oversees and manages the company in the capacity of a business coach.

Brenda completed her speaker's training with The Motivational Center with Dr. Tina Dupree. Brenda completed her coach training at Florida International University with Dr. Martha Beck. Brenda received her Life Coach Certification from the International Coaching Federation and North Star Group. Oprah Winfrey's Life Coach Expert, *New York Times* best-selling author, and *O Magazine* monthly contributor, Dr. Martha Beck, personally trained Brenda. As the beloved originator of The Royal Collection®, Brenda L. Hill-Riggins, affectionately known as "the transformation coach," fostered the emergence of an inspirational understanding from an individual perspective and has plans to watch it grow to a billion-dollar market.

Brenda is the mother of four and grandmother of eight. She is a world traveler, loves to cook and entertain, is learning how to be a farmer, and resides in beautiful Miami, Florida, with her husband, Marcus A. Riggins, and their dogs, Bear and Focus.

Brenda Hill-Riggins

Brenda L. Hill-Riggins
MARS Contractors, Inc.
www.brendalhill.com

CHAPTER NINE

An interview with...

D. Trinidad Hunt

Life Without Limits: Train Your Brain for Entrepreneurial Success

David E. Wright (Wright)

Today we're speaking with D. Trinidad Hunt. Trinidad is an International author, consultant, trainer, and keynote speaker with over thirty years of experience in the area of program development and training. She is also the co-founder of two training and consulting firms, Élan Enterprises LLC and Élan Asia-Pacific as well as World Youth Network International, a non-profit organization for youth.

As co-founder of Élan Enterprises LLC, Trinidad was acknowledged in the *International Who's Who of Professional and Business Women.* As a training developer, Trinidad has written programs for business leaders both nationally and internationally for companies such as Pepsi Cola, Frito Lay, Sprint, and The Royal Bank of Canada. As a result of her expertise in business and leadership, Trinidad has been invited to speak in Australia, China, India, Canada, and the Philippines.

Trinidad hosted her own radio talk show on the East Coast in the United States. Trin's work includes executive coaching as well as the development of in-house corporate management programs. Today, she is often asked to speak on one of her newest models of Intellectual, Emotional, and Social (IQ, EQ, SQ) balance and how it affects leadership in the twenty-first century.

Wright

It's nice to be with you again, Trin.

D. Trinidad Hunt (Trin)

It's really good to speak with you, David. It's been almost a year since we last connected and the most amazing thing happened for me during that time. It felt as if our conversation remained in my head and at various intervals, new insights or thoughts would pop into my mind. It was like having an ongoing dialogue with you—an open-ended conversation centered on success in business and in life. Our conversation opened with the discussion chronicled in the book *Roadmap to Success* and now we're dropping in for the sequel.

Wright

Only this time we're focused on the entrepreneurial spirit, and instead of holding a dialogue in your head, I'll be here for the discussion!

Trin

That's right, David.

Wright

Well then, let me pose a question to you, Trin. Do you really believe that there is such a thing as the *"entrepreneurial spirit"*?

Trin

Absolutely, David! Just as we might think of Tiger Woods, Venus Williams, or Michael Phelps as having a "competitive spirit," so I believe there is an entrepreneurial spirit. If you look at the literature, quite a bit has been said about this entrepreneurial spirit.

But I don't believe there are the "haves" and "have not's" in this domain. I think we can all improve on and enhance our sense of independence and creativity, whether we work within a company or we start our own companies.

Wright

So having an entrepreneurial spirit doesn't necessarily mean that you'll start your own business?

Trin

Absolutely not! In my particular case, the process of starting my own business happened as a natural progression. But I've coached others who have shifted their approach to their work within an organization, moved up in an organization, or changed organizations. Of course, there are others who have started their own businesses.

In any and all of these cases, it begins with inner perturbation. People experience a sense of discontent and a desire to grow. The key is to find a "fit" or match that people can grow into. Once they have expanded to fill their roles or positions by mastering the challenges at that level, these people often feel that discontent again until they find the next place to expand into. From my experience, it's a spiraling sequence—*Perturbation and Discontent—Expansion and Growth—Achievement and Satisfaction—Constriction and Discontent.*

I think we're intellectually aware that life is a process but sometimes when our expectations and desires aren't being immediately met, we lose touch with that. The result is often frustration rather than patience with the process.

In the light of this, I'd like to approach this subject from the aspect of process rather than product. In other words, I thought we might look at the entrepreneurial spirit from the process of growth and expansion. What are some of the signposts or markers along the path? And even more importantly, how can we direct and redirect our energies toward greater satisfaction, fulfillment, and contribution as we progress along the path?

Wright

So our discussion will help people who want to enhance this "entrepreneurial spirit," no matter where they are.

Trin

An unequivocal, *yes!* And this includes those who already are entrepreneurs. Because we're approaching entrepreneurship from the vantage point of process, I'll include a few exercises at the back of this chapter that will help anyone at any level in his or her expansion process. These exercises will support people in clarifying, re-clarifying, and strengthening their success, satisfaction, and service ratio as they move through life. I recommend that those I coach do them periodically, depending on the stage they are going through in their business and personal lives.

Wright

That sounds great, Trin. And of course, our readers have told us that they love doing the inventories and activities, so we'll gladly include the exercises at the back of this chapter.

Trin

As I look back over the landscape of my life thus far, David, certain internal markers become visible just beneath the surface of my daily activities. I'd like to cover five of these markers today. The first is something I call Divine Discontent because it is about the natural innate desire to grow and expand. The second marker is Purpose and Passion. The third is something I call Shape Shifting which I'll share in detail as we go along. And the final two markers are Train Your Brain and Excellence in Action.

Wright

Great! Let's begin.

Trin

My earliest awareness of this burgeoning enterprising spirit was not a comfortable one. It began with a feeling of unrest, a sense of discontent, an underlying angst that had, in its early stages, no real focal point. Instead, it began as a general malaise with the state of the world and more specifically, the state of *my* own world.

Looking back now, it was as if this inner agitation or perturbation grew in intensity until it caused a fissure in my mind and heart. It was as if I didn't fit in my own skin anymore. I was teaching at the time. But what had earlier given me great pleasure no longer burned brightly or satisfied my soul. New life was pressing into consciousness, and the first sign of this life was extreme discomfort.

Back then, I had neither the ability nor the maturity to separate myself from my experience so that I could view it more objectively. Had I been able to distance myself from these feelings, I might have recognized them for what they were—the next stage of life unfolding. Instead, I felt as if I *was* my experience. I *was* the discomfort. I *was* the angst and the restlessness. Because I couldn't separate myself from my experience, these feelings of dissatisfaction built up for months before they turned into a conscious longing, a hunger, and a thirst for something more.

Marker #1—Divine Discontent

Today as a life coach and professional consultant, I've learned to recognize and identify this discontent for what it is: a *divine discontent*. Life was exerting itself—the natural inclination to grow was breaking forth through the old worn-out forms, forms that no longer served me.

It reminds me of the tiny stalks of green pushing through the six-inch rock wall that borders my pool. When I first had the wall built, it looked like solid, impenetrable rock. But within a few months, tiny green shoots began to show themselves between the chinks and crevices of stone. Seedlings of every kind had sprouted. Each sprout seeking the light, forging its own path through any tiny fracture it could find.

My rock wall is a mere microcosm of the life force in action. Although I travel all over the world for speaking engagements, I call Hawaii my home. Actually, I live on the Big Island of Hawaii. Because of this, I've had the opportunity to meet geologists who come here from all over the world to study the birth of new land. This is one of the rare places in the world where scientists can observe and monitor every part of Earth's life cycle, beginning with lava pushing up from the seabed floor.

Here geologists can track the entire process as lava forms new land and ultimately, over time, begins to decompose due to seedlings forcing their way through the hard volcanic crust breaking it down into soil. This process is the process of life. Every solid lava crust eventually gives way to shoots and shrubs as new life demands its time in the sun. Life itself pushes outward and upward, refusing to be stopped.

Today, when people come to me for coaching it is often because this inner turmoil, or perturbation, has begun. The first step in the process is to help them view these feelings of unrest as a positive sign. It is *"life without limits"* pushing through again. This perspective is very freeing for most people. As they reinterpret, re-label, or reframe their experience in a positive light, they can view their angst and malaise as healthy dissatisfaction.

The signs and signals of inner upheaval can now be viewed as divine discontent. New life is pushing up against the crusty surface of the old. New seeds in the form of ideas, needs, desires, or propensities are beginning to sprout, seeking the light of this person's attention.

With this reframe, there is a release of energy marked by a "felt shift" in awareness. The energy of resistance dissipates and the "flow state," characterized by a sense of joy or freedom, becomes available. Flow state is that high performance energy state in which the activity itself, in this case breaking through to clarity, is experienced as intrinsically rewarding. The individual can now move on much more quickly to manifest the next phase in his or her growth and development.

Wright

I can even feel the release as you speak, Trin. It's like a long slow exhale, as if I can relax and let the process take its course.

Trin

Well that's it, David. Once that felt shift occurs, we can "let go and let life." This is usually accompanied by a sense of "allowing" a feeling of riding the wave rather than being caught in it. We release any tightness or "trying to handle" or trying to manage or control our discomfort. We breathe a little more deeply and there is a sense of peaceful acceptance as we begin to trust the process of life once more. This acceptance is usually accompanied by a heightened sense of being connected to our own "true self," our inner core.

My own experience with it is it's as if there is a rush of energy. What was once blocked begins to flow. Others have told me it is like the experience of coming home to themselves—a sense of being in harmony, as though they are on track with their lives again.

So marker number one is restlessness or discontent. And the antidote for it is reframing our experience and realizing that life works if we will only get out of the way and let it. From this vantage point we can move forward.

Wright

Many people have spoken of "reframing," but as we were talking, I had a direct experience of it. There's a sense of freedom, of moving beyond constriction.

Trin

You're right, David. That's the power of reframing our experience. It allows us to move forward in the flow state. This ability to reframe is a critical skill for the entrepreneur in that it gives the individual the ability to shift from a myopic vision to an expanded perspective.

It's the eagle's view rather than the frog's. The frog sees the edge of the lily pad he's sitting on, the water surrounding him, and maybe even the shore before him. The eagle, on the other hand, sees the frog on the lily pad, the entire pond, and the landscape beyond. The eagle's view is an expanded view. This expanded perspective opens up a myriad of choices. It gives the eagle the freedom to choose both his flight path and landing site.

It is the same with the entrepreneur or anyone for that matter. Once people learn to reframe their experience, they gain a powerful tool that they can use in almost any challenging situation. When they feel trepidation or fear, for example, they can reframe their fear as False Evidence Appearing Real.

When we are stuck in fear or trepidation of any kind, we feel small and disconnected from our source—disassociated. When we transcend the fear or angst through reframing, we experience the long slow exhale you spoke about. We shift from the short constricted view to the long expanded view. By letting go, we get back in touch with our natural inner resilience, creativity and resourcefulness as well as our ability to manage ourselves and move through any change that may show up in our lives.

Wright

Okay, so once we experience this inner discontent and reframe our experience, then what?

Trin

As we acknowledge the discontent and recognize it for what it is, we can move on to the next marker. This next internal marker is accompanied by a growing awareness—a longing or desire to do something. It is a driving and motivating energetic force as if it was the electrical current that ignites the fire in the heart of each of us.

Wright

Well that's powerful! And what is the second marker again?

Trin

It's the marker of Purpose and Passion, for I have not been able to separate the two.

Marker #2—Purpose and Passion

Actually, David, our purpose and passion as well as our gifts and talents seem to be inextricably bound. It's as if each and every one of us is on a journey. We have all acquired a means of travel, known as our body, and we each come equipped with specific gifts and talents. These gifts and talents reveal themselves as natural inclinations of the soul. Together our passion, our purpose, our gifts, and our talents galvanize our energies and spur us into action.

In many of the Native American traditions, it was believed that each person was born with gifts and talents and that these were to be used in service to the tribe. Every person had a special role to play within the tribe based on the talents each received at birth. Only he or she could fulfill that role, for only that specific person came fully equipped to do so. Each life was viewed as purposeful; every person fit perfectly into the whole of society or the tribe.

So it is with us today. Our own joy and happiness is intrinsically tied to what we ardently love to do, what we passionately enjoy. When we are passionate, we are naturally more energetic, enthusiastic, inspired, and animated. What we are truly passionate about excites and engages us fully and is in turn connected to the full expression of our natural gifts and talents. It's as if we were born to express our "selves"—born to share our special and unique gifts and talents within the "tribe" or our greater community.

I happen to have been a student and a great fan of the late Joseph Campbell. He always spoke of our lives as a great mythic adventure. "The big question," he used to say, "is whether you are going to be able to say a hearty yes to your adventure."

Your bliss is your passion. Your passion and your gifts are purposeful. They make up the invisible thread that can be followed to your natural path of full self-expression.

Wright

But you have just set before us a conundrum, Trin! You've given us a dilemma of sorts! How does a person follow a thread that's not visible? How do we get in touch with what is not seen?

Trin

That's where the exercises at the back of this section come in. Each exercise was designed to shine the light of consciousness into areas we may have been only dimly aware of. Each exercise will reveal a portion or an aspect of your inner landscape—your inner reality.

The exercises require a bit of self-reflection. Each activity will ask you to reflect on your experience from a certain vantage point. One activity will ask you to reflect back on moments in your life when you felt most alive—when you felt your best and happiest. Another will ask you to move forward along your time line and look back on your life to what you did and what you contributed, while another will invite you to mind-map your ideal self.

Each of these written exercises will reveal a portion of the thread that leads to the core of why you're here and what you've come to do. It is both a personal and transpersonal experience in which you lose your small self-identity and feel yourself "in flow" once more.

Wright

Great. It sounds as if the exercises will make it much easier for people to get in touch with that "invisible thread" as you call it.

Trin

Not only that, David, but I've also done these exercises myself as well as used them in training programs for over thirty years. So they come pre-tested. Participants have told me how easy the exercises are to do and how exhilarating it feels when they start to get back in touch with the thread of their own lives.

Many of these people went on to start their own businesses. However, there were others who didn't feel an inclination to do that. These people said they felt an expanded sense of ownership regarding the businesses they were in. These people often went on to head departments or to expand the departments that they headed within a larger organization. They created an opportunity for growth within the company of their choice. The exercises will help people in achieving greater clarity for themselves.

By the way, I recommend that a person do these exercises again after a few years. Personally, I've done them at least a dozen times at varying intervals in my life. Whenever I feel that "divine discontent" breaking through, I know that it's time to re-evaluate. These exercises have helped me focus and refocus, then set my course and course-correct as I move through the process of my own life expansion.

Wright

Now you've gotten me excited. But our readers might be thinking that there's an age limit to all of this.

Trin

No way, David, I'm personally going through another life change, so I recently did the exercises again myself. As a result, I'm moving into another level of expansion as we speak.

Besides, David, if you're on the planet, you're here for a reason. Each and every one of us who is here on Earth has something yet to do. Maybe I can clarify what I mean by this by moving to the next marker. I call this marker *shape-shifting*.

Marker #3—"Shape-shifting"

If you follow your passion, you'll shape-shift your brain! As you probably know, "shape-shifting" refers to a mythological physical change from one form to another, such as an animal into a human or vice versa. It would be the term used, for example, to describe the "frog into a prince" idea that we so often see in children's stories. This is perfectly exemplified in the famous children's tale, "Beauty and the Beast" when the beast is transformed by the love of the princess into the handsome prince that he really was.

This type of physical shape-shifting is a common theme in the fairy tales and in myths of almost every culture down through time. But I'm going to use the term to represent a complete and irrevocable transformation of the mind, and a critical step on the path to entrepreneurship.

My own experience of shape-shifting took place over a period of approximately three years. I always had a natural affinity for exceptional performance. It didn't matter whether it was in the area of the arts and sciences, or sports, or leadership and business—any person who made any major contribution in any field interested me. During my early twenties while teaching in San Diego, I became a voracious reader devouring every biography and autobiography I could get my hands on. I was fascinated by the mindset and emotional stamina of successful people.

As I read the works of different people and studied their lives and the way they thought, my mind began to go through a change. But it wasn't until much later in looking back, that I realized the degree of "shape-shifting" my brain had undergone during that phase of my life.

Rather than a change in my physical shape, I had gone through a change in my mental state. It was a metamorphosis of the mind that I had experienced. In fact, I had changed so completely that my new self barely recognized my old.

Little did I know at that time that within two years, through a series of unexpected events, my avocation would become my vocation. Joseph Campbell was spot on when he said, "Follow your bliss and the universe will open doors where there were only walls." My passion had become a lightening rod, attracting to me people and events that would open doors for me.

It came to me in the form of an invitation to join a training company, which I did. Eighteen months later the CEO called me in and asked me to buy the company from him, which I did. And the rest, as they say, is history. I sold the company later but it was this company that became the springboard for my moving into training, coaching, and speaking nationally and internationally.

For any of us, shape-shifting of the mind occurs as a result of following and becoming absorbed in what we are naturally drawn to or love. In my case, the transformation occurred as a result of being passionately fascinated with outstanding performance and great success.

So the point is, David, attention equals energy. As we put our attention on what we love and become completely immersed in, the brain itself begins to undergo a change. Ultimately, "where we put our attention is where we get the result." This complete immersion leads to higher order restructuring. The exercises we're included in the back of this chapter will help people do that. Essentially, they will help people break through the old outmoded mindset or belief system that kept them operating at one level and help them break through to the next level.

Wright

Obviously, the implications of this are exciting for everyone. But, specifically, how do you see this concept of "shape-shifting" specifically empowering and supporting entrepreneurs today?

Trin

Well for myself, David, I wasn't born an entrepreneur. Like everyone else on the planet, I came in with gifts and talents. But I wasn't born to do business. Instead, as I read of the lives and thinking of high achievers, my brain went through a radical contextual shift. Then I had to support that shift by "up-skilling" my brain. I had to train my brain with the qualities of the highly successful. Then I had to make these attitudes and this mindset automatic. I had to turn them into habits. But this leads to the next marker.

Marker #4—Train Your Brain

I'd like to preface this marker by sharing an incident that happened at the time of my writing my first book. I had a long-term training contract with the Kona Surf in Hawaii. Knowing that I was writing, the manager, Ned Nedderson, gave me a suite overlooking the ocean. "The vast expanse of the sea will inspire you," he said as he walked me through the six-hundred-and-fifty-foot suite perched on the edge of the sea.

Ned was right. I spent three days a week in training and the other three days writing. I usually took Sundays off and it was on one of those Sundays during the month of the Kona Triathlon that I met a young man at the hotel pool. He was tall with long sinewy limbs and it was therefore no surprise when told me that he had been training for the triathlon for over a year.

His name was Mike and he said he'd arrived the day before from the mile-high city of Denver. "It's my first triathlon," he said. "I heard all kinds of stories about the humidity of the air at sea level. So not knowing what to expect, I came in a week early to prepare my body and especially my lungs for the drastic change in altitude."

Mike was right—Kona is known for being hot and its air sultry. Most tri-athletes try an easier course than Kona for their first go. "This is your first go at it?" I queried, a bit taken aback.

"I thought I'd push the envelope a bit," he smiled reflectively. "If I can finish in Kona, any other place in the world will be a cake-walk for me."

Mike and I spent the next half hour talking about his year of preparation for the event. As we talked, I realized that what he was sharing was no different from the strengthening of the entrepreneurial spirit in business. The end result was different—an athletic event on the one hand, and business on the other. But the process of development was similar.

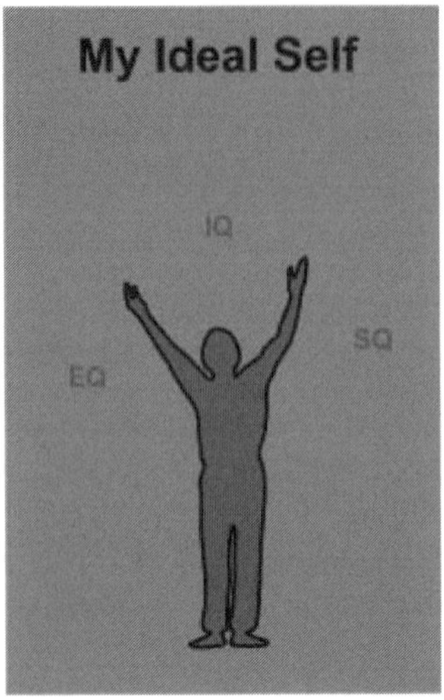

He spoke of the mindset he had to develop and talked about how a big part of his training was building the mental and emotional stamina for the long haul. What he shared was identical to the mental and emotional stamina that each of us has to develop in order to be successful in the field of our choice.

No matter what their profession or field of choice, people must *train their brain for success.* Here we use an exercise for developing and/or enhancing the qualities and characteristics of those who are very successful. We call it the Ideal Self exercise.

We use the IQ, EQ SQ Model™ for this exercise. When you look at the picture, IQ stands for Intellectual Qualities, EQ stands for Emotional Qualities, and SQ stands for Social Qualities. Again, we have included this activity at the back of the chapter. Essentially, we ask people to write on the front of the card the qualities, characteristics, and attributes that they want to develop or enhance in themselves. While we use a specially designed card for those we coach, anyone can do this exercise on a three-inch by five-inch or four-inch by six-inch card.

This activity forms a visual template for the future. Then we ask people to focus on this picture, enhancing the vision of their ideal self with sensory rich feelings of success.

Wright

That's quite a concept! It sounds like the IQ, EQ SQ Model and the exercise to enhance those different qualities would be a great for anyone in leadership, or even in life.

Trin

Absolutely, David. About ten months ago, I was cleaning out my office and I found a faded, tattered, yellow Post-it Note stuck between two books on my bookshelf. As I pulled the sticky note from the back of one of the books and read the words, a wash of memories flooded back.

I had penciled this note to myself in my mid-thirties. After writing my Who's Who and doing all of the other exercises, I had culled it down to the five things I really wanted to accomplish before I left the planet.

As I read the faded words, the joy that washed over me was almost inexpressible. I realized that I had accomplished all but one item on the list. And the one that was left was a lifetime goal. It's in process now, but it will take my entire lifetime to complete. Everything else I said that I would do, I had done.

Wright

That must be an incredible feeling!

Trin

Absolutely, a shiver of exhilaration flushed through me, David. It was as if I was right on track with my promise to myself and to God.

Wright

That's remarkable. So I guess what you're saying is that these exercises in the back of this section are life-changing.

Trin

You're right—totally life-changing for myself as well thousands of others I've worked with. And the five items on my list weren't small goals either; they were my five "big-ticket" purpose and passion items.

I guess the other thing is that the exercises I'm sharing in the back of this chapter don't have to be done all at once. I invite our readers to try them over a one-week time frame so there is time to integrate the results.

I do know they work because of the results I've had with them both personally and with those I coach. But I'm not asking people to believe me. I invite our readers to try them for themselves and to have fun with them. They are actually fun to do.

So! The markers I have shared thus far are all the inner territory. The final marker is the outer territory. It is the marker of taking action in the world.

Wright

This is where it all culminates, of course!

Trin

Exactly! As every entrepreneur knows, you have to act. This is where all the habits and all the inner training kick in.

For Mike, our tri-athlete, it was where the mental practice turned into physical practice. It was literally where the "rubber hit the road" for Mike. It's also the reason he decided to do the Kona triathlon before any other easier course. He said that he wanted to put his inner training to the ultimate test.

So our final marker is about taking action. We call it *excellence in action*. This is about developing not just the mental and emotional habits but also the daily habits of the successful entrepreneur.

Wright

That makes me think of the "Miracle on the Hudson" story, Trin. I mean, the outcome of Captain Sullenberger's landing his crippled plane on the Hudson River and saving everyone on board was a first in aviation history. Isn't that the kind of outcome you're talking about—where the mind-set, the passion, and the action become one to produce a "text-book landing"?

Trin

It was exactly that, David! Captain Sullenberger's engines went out about a minute after takeoff when he ran into a flock of birds. At three thousand feet he had to make a decision: return to La Guardia Airport or find another place to land the plane. Captain Sullenberger's incredible ability to remain calm under pressure is really an example of both inner and outer training.

If you go back in time and follow Captain Sullenberger's life, it is a clear example of what we've been talking about. It was said that Sully (as his friends called him) had spent his entire life in preparation for this event. His sister said he used to build model airplanes as a youngster. At fourteen Sully became a pilot and as an adult he went on to fly in the Air Force.

But talk about "shape-shifting" it didn't stop there! Captain Sullenberger went on to study the psychology of crises behavior in the cockpit and even investigated air disasters. At one point in the news clip, his wife said that her husband loved the "art of the plane." Over the years, his passion and his practice became habit and that habit paid off for the one hundred and fifty passengers aboard flight 1549 on that January day in 2009.

But there's one more amazing thing that fits this picture perfectly, David.

Wright

What's that, Trin?

Trin

Well it turns out that Captain Sullenberger is the CEO of his own company called Safety Reliability Methods, Inc. This is a classic case of everything we have been talking about. Here is a man who turned his avocation into his vocation. Need I say more? The final marker is *excellence in action*.

Marker #5—Excellence in Action

The final marker is the marker of execution—how we go about our work and take action to achieve our purpose. Here one has the opportunity to manifest one's passion through daily behaviors and practices. For the entrepreneur, self-management, or time and energy management, is the keystone to success.

Obviously, the things to do on a daily basis will be different for each one of us. Our tasks will match our purpose and passion. However, there are some overarching practices that have helped me stay on target with my purpose while remaining flexible and receptive to the synchronicities that the day may bring.

Tune in and Tune up

My day begins with my own personal spiritual practice. This includes a few moments of gratitude for what I have and then about half an hour of quiet meditation or prayer. This is a very personal time for every one of us. For myself, I've found that it sets the tone for my entire day. As a result, I encourage those I coach to set some early morning time aside to tune into their Higher Source.

I added an artist's palette to symbolize the next portion of my practice. I usually close my quiet time with a two-part visualization. First, I visualize myself being the ideal self that I have written on my card. Then I see my ideal self going through the coming day. This is a short mental walk-through of the things I'm going to do and the people I am going to meet with that day. I see the day and all activities flowing smoothly as I operate from my highest ideal.

Purpose & Passion

While my energy tends to be quite consistent throughout the day, my peak time is in the morning. Because of this, I target my "big ticket" purpose and passion items during this morning stretch. For myself, this includes everything that requires a high degree of focus and concentration. Also, if I'm working on a writing project; a good night's sleep and an early morning start usually helps my writing flow.

Obviously, everyone's morning tasks will change based on their life work at that time. Yet the simple rule of thumb is to notice your energy and design your day so that your high energy peaks match your high priority purpose items.

Key Support Items

For myself, this includes anything and everything on my To-Do List that supports my long-term objectives. The afternoon usually flows easily out of my morning and the only crucial key is to get all of my high priority to-do items done by the end of the day.

Close the Day

I use the last five to ten minutes of my working day to bring a sense of closure to this part of my day. I check off and finalize everything that's complete and transfer anything that's incomplete to a new day. This includes making a quick overall assessment of the breadth of my progress toward my objectives.

Exercise, Play, Family, Friends

I usually exercise before dark with either an afternoon walk or swim in the pool, and by the end of the day, I've earned my play. The evening is such a personal time for everyone. I encourage people to celebrate a day well done by spending the evening relaxing with family and friends.

Reflect & Review

This is my "moment before the mirror." It is a time to look at how I did with my ideal self and my IQ, EQ, SQ intentions for the day. I have an electric toothbrush that ends its cycle at exactly two minutes. So my reflection begins when I pick up my toothbrush. Two minutes is exactly what I need to ask and answer my closing day questions. *What worked? What could have worked better? And where do I want to improve tomorrow?* This sets the stage for my next day.

Of course, it's always important to keep a life balance with all of the elements of work, play, and family. But essentially, that's my work week in a nutshell. That's sort of a rough sketch of how it is for me and those I coach. Each person can fill in the details for themselves.

But the final thing is to remember to be flexible. This is not meant to be a rigid process. I always recommend that people design their day to match their energies and goals. The key is, however, to be as congruent as possible by aligning words and actions. Do what you say you're going to do and be what you say you want to be.

So there it is, David. The five markers to constant improvement in the area of business and in life: follow the thread of divine discontent, purpose, and passion. Then shape-shift your mind and train your brain for success. And finally, go for excellence in action!

Wright

We've covered a lot in our short time together, Trin!

Trin

Well, there's so much more, David. But I think that what we've covered is a good overview of the process of developing and enhancing the entrepreneurial spirit.

I guess the final thing I'd like to close with is a quote from one of my small inspirational books. *Remember, your life is your sacred adventure. Nobody else can do your life as well as you can, so enjoy the journey!*

Wright

That's a good reminder, Trin, and as always, you've left us with a lot to think about. And this time you've left us with some powerful activities to do. Thank you, Trin, it's been great talking with you!

Trin

It's been great talking with you again, David. Thank *you*, I always enjoy our conversations.

The following exercises will help you more fully clarify your purpose, passion, and gifts and talents. Set about two hours aside to do them or do them at different intervals. In either case, allow yourself some quiet time with pen or pencil and four or five sheets of paper. Soft, unobtrusive background music is also helpful but not imperative for setting the scene. Immerse yourself in your inner vision and enjoy.

Exercise for Marker #2: Passion

Exercise #1: If my life were absolutely perfect, I would be . . .

Take a deep breath. Gently hold it for a few seconds and then let it out. Again, breathe, hold, and release. Imagine yourself now rising above the landscape of your life. Notice the peaks and valleys that stretch back as far as you can see.

Now, focus your inner vision on the high points. Notice the times when you felt most inspired, energetic, happy, and even joyful. What were you doing at that time? Who were you with and how did you feel at that time?

Then open your eyes and make a list of ten to fifteen items that start with the following: *If my life were absolutely perfect, I would be . . .*

When you feel complete, choose your top five "big ticket items." These would be the most important items on the list—the ones that will give you the greatest satisfaction.

Exercise for Marker #2: Purpose

Exercise #2: Who's Who

Take a deep breath. Gently hold it for a few seconds and then let it out. Again, breathe, hold, and release. Do this a few times, and as you do, allow your eyes to close.

Imagine now that you are ninety-seven years of age. You are sitting at your desk in your study looking at the landscape beyond your window.

You have lived a rich, full, and rewarding life. There is a glow of health, an aura of energy around you. You have in your lifetime become fully self-actualized. You are energetic and mentally clear. There is an aura of peace around you and a sense of wisdom about you.

The phone rings and you answer it. The voice on the other end introduces himself as the editor of *Who's Who in* __________ *(America, Canada, Australia, Singapore,* etc. your country).* He asks you if you will write a short article on yourself, highlighting the following things:

What have you done in your life?

What do you want to be remembered for?

If you could have your name be synonymous with something, what would you want your name to be synonymous with? (The word "mentor" came from the name Mentor. When Ulysses, the hero of Homer's poem, *The Odyssey,* went to war, he left his son, Telemachus, in the care of Mentor. The word, "mentor" has come to mean trusted friend, adviser, or teacher.)

What kind of energy do you express? Is your energy inspiring, calm, warm, friendly, active, and energetic? What energy do people feel in your presence?

What contribution did you make to life and to the lives of those around you?

What did you give?

*Write your *Who's Who* in the third person, past tense. Imagine that you are ninety-seven, looking back and telling the story of what this person has become and what he or she has already done in life.

Possible Exercises for Marker #3: Shape-shifting

Below are a list of things that you might want to do to shape-shift your mind:

1. Do a "vision board" including all the things you want and intend for your life as you move forward to the next level. Keep this board where you can see it. Look at it every day, not as if you wish it would happen, but as if it is in process—coming to you now. Imagine that everything you want is just hanging in cyberspace waiting for the right dot com address to release it to you. Your vision board is that dot com address!
2. Read about the people who have done something you wanted to do. Immerse yourself in their thinking and their mindset. What are the qualities and characteristics that helped these people succeed?
3. Watch videos about people and situations that inspire you. There are wonderful videos available about people who have achieved great success in every area from art to science to sports to teaching.

Exercise for Marker #4: Train Your Brain

The Ideal Self Exercise:

Pick a time frame of six months to a year and imagine yourself as you would like to be. What qualities, characteristics, and skills would you like to have embodied by that time? You may want to review the earlier activities—your passion exercise, your *Who's Who,* and your vision board, if you have done one. Note the qualities and characteristics you will need to accomplish your vision. Mind-map these on the front of your card.

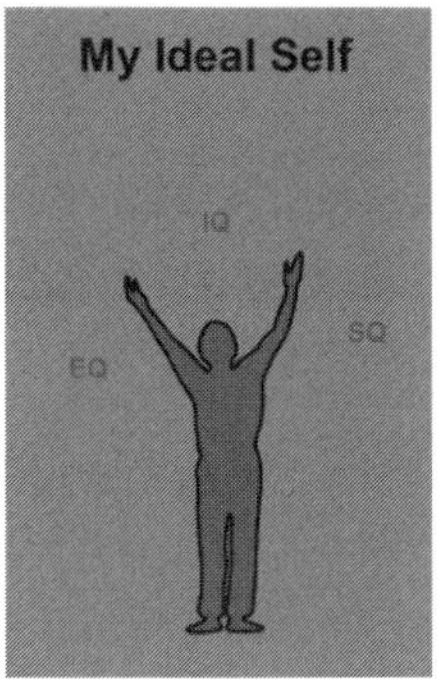

Don't be overly zealous. Start by writing one attribute in each of the IQ, EQ, SQ areas. As time goes on and you get better at this, you will probably want to do a new card. Below you will find a sample list of qualities or character traits to jump-start your thinking.

Intellectual Qualities: demonstrates mental agility, focused, uses forethought, curious, loves learning, visionary, creative, self-aware, goal-oriented

Emotional Qualities: perseveres, patient, adaptable, flexible, self-disciplined, courageous, enthusiastic, takes initiative, exhibits psychological hardiness, delays gratification for a long-term goal, willing to take calculated risks, has a sense of appreciation or gratitude, exhibits calm under pressure

Social Qualities: respectful, helpful, empathetic, considerate, easily forgives, listens, team player, considerate of others, networker, compassionate

At the base of the card, near the feet of the character, you may want to include a few of the action items you need to be successful. These might include such things as: *"rise at 5:30 AM daily," "do my daily meditation and prayer," "do five things to move me closer to my vision every day," "give thanks for what I have and who I am every day."*

Place this card on the mirror where you brush your teeth. Visualize it daily.

ABOUT THE AUTHOR

Trinidad Hunt is an International author, consultant, trainer, and keynote speaker with over thirty years of experience in the area of program development and training. She is also the co-founder of two training and consulting firms, Élan Enterprises LLC and Élan Asia-Pacific as well as World Youth Network International, a non-profit organization for youth.

As co-founder of Élan Enterprises LLC, Trinidad was acknowledged in the *International Who's Who of Professional and Business Women.* As a training developer, Trinidad has written programs for business leaders both nationally and internationally for companies such as Pepsi Cola, Frito Lay, Sprint, and The Royal Bank of Canada. As a result of her expertise in business and leadership, Trinidad has been invited to speak in Australia, China, India, Canada, and the Philippines.

Trinidad hosted her own radio talk show on the East Coast in the United States. Today, she is often asked to speak on her newest model of Intellectual, Emotional, and Social (IQ, EQ, SQ) balance and how it affects leadership in the twenty-first century.

D. Trinidad Hunt

Élan Enterprises, LLC
Élan Asia-Pacific
elantrin@aol.com
Toll free: U.S. & Canada 800-707-3526
Phone: 808-239-4431
Fax: 808-239-2482
Contact: CEO/VP, Lynne Truair
elantrin@aol.com
www.elanlearninginstitute.com
www.quest4character.com
www.endbullying.com

CHAPTER **TEN**

An interview with...

Darlene Ziebell

Building a Foundation for a Successful Business Plan

David Wright (Wright)

Today we're talking with Darlene Ziebell. Darlene has over thirty years of experience in business consulting and entrepreneurship. Through her years of owning several businesses and consulting to some of the largest companies in the world, Darlene offers a wealth of experience to the business owner. She grew a business management consulting firm from zero to over $40M in a fifteen-year period. Her methods are based on a unique blend of large enterprise strategies, battle scars earned, and experiences she had as an entrepreneur in many businesses including startups, mergers, acquisitions, and partnerships. She advises and trains business owners on successful planning and strategy through her *Empowering Entrepreneurs* workshops. Darlene is a guest speaker at various business associations and consulted to over 20 percent of Fortune 1000 companies.

Empowering Entrepreneurs is a methodology designed for owners of closely held companies. The process is designed with flexibility, size, and convenience of implementation needed by the hands-on entrepreneur. In a typical business plan, each area of business operations is included; but what major components do the *most* successful business owners include in *their* strategy? The answer is fundamental awareness of all the people associated with the business—including themselves. These are the things that Darlene teaches.

Darlene, welcome to *Bootstrap Business.*

Darlene Ziebell (Ziebell)

Thank you very much, David.

Wright

What is fundamental awareness and why is it so important to successful business planning?

Ziebell

Many businesses fail every year. There are several underlying attributes key to those business owners who are successful. These attributes are those principles, personalities and strengths that make up the individual. In a successful business plan, fundamental awareness includes an understanding of the individual business owner's personal attributes as well as key knowledge of all the people who are involved with the business including customers, vendors, suppliers, and partners.

Wright

Would you describe for our readers the underlying attributes individual entrepreneurs need to be successful?

Ziebell

Envision an architect building a house. Each room of this house represents a different business function. For example, there would be rooms for sales, marketing, finance, inventory, and distribution, depending on the type of business and the industry. But without a solid foundation, this building would collapse.

Envision the elements of fundamental awareness as the foundation of the business plan and strategy.

Wright

You state one of the attributes of fundamental awareness is for entrepreneurs to know why they are in business. Is it really important for entrepreneurs to know why they're in business to succeed?

Ziebell

If entrepreneurs understand why they're going into business, they have a much better chance of success because they will design business plans that match their reasons for going into business in the first place. If an entrepreneur has a great business idea and is very passionate about making it a success, he or she could overcome a lot of different obstacles. However, business owners get so wrapped up in the excitement of incorporating, opening their commercial bank account, getting new business cards, and designing company logos, they avoid addressing the more difficult question of the real reason they are in business.

Many business owners start their business with the premise, "If I build it, they will come," or "I have a great idea for a business and I know it will work!" If they're among the many business owners who have been talked into going into business through a partnership or maybe inheriting a business, they may not have a passionate interest in the business, and therefore not succeed. It's really important for business owners to understand why they're getting into a particular business venture.

Wright

So how can people know if they really have what it takes to succeed as business owners?

Ziebell

Business owners must measure their level of risk tolerance. Successful entrepreneurs have drive, are willing to take risks, and demonstrate great initiative to own their own business. It is important for business owners to understand themselves—how much are they willing to commit to make a business work? If they're going into it because they feel that it's just something simple to do and an easy way to make money, they may be going into it for the wrong reasons. The business plan must reflect the business owner's tolerance for financial risk and the business operations must be designed accordingly.

Wright

Passion and solid business management skills—which does an entrepreneur need?

Ziebell

The entrepreneur needs both. Why does an entrepreneur need passion? I have worked with many successful business owners who started a business in an industry in which they had absolutely no experience. They were successful because of their drive to learn whatever it would take to make the business profitable. They had passion. They knew their strengths and admitted their weaknesses. They surrounded themselves with people who could advise them on what they needed to do. They worked with other business owners to learn what they needed to know, and asked their customers, "How can we serve you better?" They began their business with sweat equity and, in some cases, still had a separate full-time career. They worked many hours every week to succeed and eventually were able to work at their own business full-time with outstanding results.

I've seen this success model many times, so I know people can own their own business if they have enough passion.

Wright

So how do entrepreneurs measure their management skills?

Ziebell

Many people start a business feeling they have the management skill and expertise needed to be successful. Many may have worked in a similar industry for a very long period of time. Understanding their level of passion and management skills are equally important. The gaps identified should be reflected as part of their business plan.

Wright

If the business owner's personal level of risk tolerance affects the success of the business, how is this risk level blended into the business planning process?

Ziebell

If business owners understand where they fall on the scale of being risk-takers versus not being risk-takers, they can design a new business or purchase an existing business based on that level of risk tolerance. For example, those with a very low financial level of risk tolerance are not going into a start-up planning to build a fifty-million-dollar company overnight. Those who want to take a low level of risk would have a better chance of success by starting a business in smaller chunks. If people understand their personal tolerance for risk before they design a business plan or strategy, they would have a much bigger chance of success.

Wright

So as you define "risk," I know you're talking mostly about financial risk. Are there other risks to consider?

Ziebell

I'm talking about financial risk and financial risk is also emotional risk. They are also taking a risk on their business knowledge—what are they really willing to commit to make a business a success? Additionally, they have to commit the time and the effort. If they're going into business for themselves because they think it's a lot easier to run one's own business versus working for someone else, they may be in for a rude awakening.

Wright

What you just said is really true for me. I had been in business by myself since the middle sixties and then all of a sudden, when I turned fifty, I had a baby coming. I thought, "Do I really need to do all this?

Ziebell

Business owners start measuring their whole life as they go through a business planning process. There are many people with great ideas for starting a new business venture, but in a business planning process, they must consider their current state of life. There are many circumstances that have to be taken into consideration if they want a business to be a success. It takes more than deciding one's financial level of risk.

Wright

So as you're helping your clients, do you go into all of these risks?

Ziebell

The methodology I designed, *Empowering Entrepreneurs,* encompasses these attributes of fundamental awareness. When I evaluate my clients' business plans, I first clarify these principles of fundamental awareness. Once these principles are identified, they become the foundation of the business plan.

Wright

Back in the sixties, when I started my first business, I wish I'd had the advantage of *Empowering Entrepreneurs.*

Ziebell

I've learned this process through many years of trial and error. I've taken all the experience from consulting to Fortune 1000 companies and the experience of owning my own businesses, and evaluated what worked and what didn't work. From that, I developed a business-planning process for owners of closely held companies.

Wright

So this is not just theory.

Ziebell

Absolutely not. I apply these methods to my current businesses. This process will work for the experienced business owner or those testing the entrepreneur process for the first time.

Wright

So how do these underlying attributes affect a business with more than one owner, such as a partnership?

Ziebell

Each business partner comes into a business relationship with a different set of fundamental principles that need to be taken into consideration—especially if there are more than two owners in the partnership. I've worked with many businesses where there are four business partners and each was at a different level.

It's key for all to agree on what fundamental principles they're following for their business strategy because they will see the results in the successful operation of their company. This is where the rubber meets the road. Many partnerships agree on a nice business strategy and plan, but sometimes they operate the business based on their own individual principles. That's where dissention and failure begin.

Wright

What are the basic principles of fundamental awareness for other people associated with the company?

Ziebell

This is the area where knowing the value of everyone who's involved in the company is important. This is the value chain. Business owners need an understanding of all the fundamental awareness principles involved with all the employees, suppliers, vendors, and the entire business distribution network. The business has a greater chance for success if everyone involved has the same principles that the company's strategy is based on. If there is a huge disconnect in principle, there is a greater chance of failure.

Wright

Why is it important for a business owner to know how customers feel when they're making a purchase?

Ziebell

Business owners must understand why customers return to buy a product or service. Whether a business sells to other businesses or sells to consumers, these same principles apply. Customers return for one of three reasons:

- Best product or service
- Best customer service
- Best price.

Every successful business is great at one of these strategic attributes and good at a second strategic attribute. But, a successful company does not manage their business using all three of these strategic attributes. Every owner must understand which of these three reasons customers return to buy a product or service. When a business chases all three of these strategic attributes, there is less chance of success. The most successful businesses in the world will be great at one attribute and good at a second, but will never follow all three. It is imperative for business owners to understand what their customers buy. Many business owners think they know, but often, those who fail don't have that understanding.

Wright

Money versus value—which is the most important in a successful business?

Ziebell

As a customer purchasing a product or service, which is more important to you: money or value? You would probably answer value. And value is not always measured by better price in exchange for a product or service. Customers may base their purchase on factors other than prices. Such factors include: safety, pride in ownership, quality, ease of purchase, ease of use, and/or many more.

Every business owner is looking for money—the only way to achieve success is to have cash flow and profitability. But what's important to the customer is value and business owners have to understand their customers' perception of value when they're designing their business plan or strategy. They must provide evidence of this value to their customers in the selling process. Companies that sell more value have a much greater chance of success.

Wright

When do you turn down a sale?

Ziebell

During times of economic downturns, many businesses chase any customer who offers to buy. However, at what price do they chase these customers? Is it important for them to accept any customer or is it more important to focus on what they sell and what they do best and wait for the market to catch up?

During a recession, there are many opportunities to start a new business, especially if creating a business model as the best low-cost provider. However, if a business model is that of providing the best quality or best customer service, that business cannot also be the low-cost provider and continue to be a success. Review the value statement to determine when to turn down a sale.

Wright

How are these principles included in a business plan or strategy?

Ziebell

First-time business owners purchase a business-planning book or software that provides them with the components of strategy and a business plan. In their next step, they may plug in some numbers. However, before they start this process, they should evaluate the principles we're talking about here and consider each when designing their business plan. This foundation will give them a much better chance to succeed.

Wright

So if I attended one of these *Empowering Entrepreneurs* workshops and learned these principles, is there a way to get in touch with you and see if I'm on track over time?

Ziebell

Yes. *Empowering Entrepreneurs* is a process where business owners look at their company as a living entity. It moves, it changes, it's alive, 24/7. Whether or not the company is nine to five, something is always happening in the world that's going to affect the business. Understanding business as a living entity is especially important today in a global marketplace.

Successful business owners know what's happening at all times and constantly reevaluate their plan. Their plan must have specific measurements allow flexibility to make strategic decisions. It is important they stay in touch with me through the implementation of their plan. I offer opportunities for continued interaction with me.

Wright

Will applying these principles help make my business a success in a difficult economy?

Ziebell

Applying these principles in a strategy or plan will make the business owner a success in any economy, including one that is in a recession. I follow these principles and I've owned five companies throughout my entrepreneur career. The companies that were the most successful were the ones I started during a recession. My methods give a business owner the opportunity to make decisions based on solid information versus decisions based on fear. During a recession, many existing companies follow a strategic plan based on fear of losing a business versus a strategy on how to succeed in an economic downturn. Understanding these principles gives a startup business owner a competitive advantage.

Wright

Well, what an interesting conversation. This is a great topic; I could talk with you about it all day. Our readers are going to learn a lot.

Ziebell

This is just the tip of the iceberg—this is all I can get into one chapter. I offer hands-on workshops where business owners can learn to apply these techniques.

Wright

Well, they can always call you.

Ziebell

Yes, and that's what I want them to do. Once business owners use these principles to create the foundation for their business plan, they'll avoid pitfalls and experience greater success.

Wright

I really appreciate the time you've taken with me this morning to answer all these questions, especially in this economic climate. We just have to do things right. So I really appreciate your giving us even just the tip of the iceberg here.

Ziebell

Well, thank you very much, David.

Wright

Today we've been talking with Darlene Ziebell. Darlene is a speaker, trainer and consultant. She's passionate about *Empowering Entrepreneurs,* which is a methodology designed specifically for owners of closely held companies. As we have found today, these methods are a unique blend of the latest large enterprise business strategies with flexibility, size and convenience of implementation needed for hands-on business owners—guys like me.

Darlene, thank you so much for being with us today on *Bootstrap Business.*

Ziebell

You're welcome.

ABOUT THE AUTHOR

Darlene has over thirty years of experience in business consulting and entrepreneurship. Through her years of owning several businesses and consulting to some of the largest companies in the world, Darlene offers a wealth of experience to the business owner. She grew a business management consulting firm from zero to over $40M in a fifteen-year period. Her methods are based on a unique blend of large enterprise strategies, battle scars earned, and experiences she had as an entrepreneur in many businesses including startups, mergers, acquisitions, and partnerships. She advises and trains business owners on successful planning and strategy through her *Empowering Entrepreneurs* workshops. Darlene is a guest speaker at various business associations and consulted to over 20 percent of Fortune 1000 companies.

Empowering Entrepreneurs is a methodology designed for owners of closely held companies. The process is designed with flexibility, size, and convenience of implementation needed by the hands-on entrepreneur. In a typical business plan, each area of business operations is included; but what major components do the *most* successful business owners include in *their* strategy? The answer is fundamental awareness of all the people associated with the business—including themselves. These are the things that Darlene teaches.

Darlene Ziebell

869 E. Schaumburg Rd., Suite 345
Schaumburg, IL 60194
847-622-9400
info@ziebellenterprises.com
www.empoweringentrepreneurs.biz

CHAPTER ELEVEN

An interview with...

John Christensen

The Fish! Philosophy® Inspiring an Engaged Workplace

David Wright (Wright)

Today we are talking with John Christensen. John's story begins in the shipping department at ChartHouse Learning where he began working as a teenager for his father, Ray. He worked his way to the top the old fashioned way, having to prove to his father and the company that he was a real filmmaker who could tell moving stories.

Today Mr. Christensen guides ChartHouse as "playground director"—business talk for CEO—with an inspiring vision of an engaged workplace that can be developed through the "*FISH! Philosophy*®." ChartHouse Learning is changing the way business is done worldwide. As his dad before him, John created an eloquent language to transform lives. In 1997, he translated what happens daily at Seattle's world famous Pike Place Fish Market's culture into a vital global learning program called FISH! and changed the entire business film industry. In the process, John also achieved his lifelong dream of how to turn workplaces into energetic, creative, and wholehearted endeavors with the four simple principles embodied in the FISH! Philosophy.

John Christensen, welcome to *Bootstrap Business.*

John Christensen (Christensen)

Thank you, David. I appreciate that.

Wright

John, obviously, my first question is what are the four simple principles of the FISH! Philosophy?

Christensen

The four simple principles are play, make their day, be there, and choose your attitude.

Wright

Play? In other words we're supposed to play at work?

Christensen

Yes. Play is the basis of where creativity and innovation happens. And if you look back into your own life and see where you were most creative, it was in those moments of play and inspiration where you got lost in the moment. We call that "play." Now if corporations are scared by that, think of it as "lightheartedness." Think of it as taking your work seriously, but take yourself lightheartedly.

Wright

So tell us a little bit about what you do at ChartHouse Learning.

Christensen

We are like cultural anthropologists. We study things that are out in the world, then we help put a language to it. For instance, that's what I saw at the fish market.

I saw these fishmongers being totally engaged in their work and I thought, "Wait a minute! Wait a minute! There's something deeper going on than just play and all this craziness that I see on the shop floor." So we interpret that, then put a language around things, and helped get it out into the business world. It's not only in the business world, schools are using it, too.

Wright

When you say "language," you're talking about terms that can be understood universally?

Christensen

Yes, absolutely. In FISH! it's ancient wisdom that's been resurfaced and presented in a new way and in an unlikely place—a fish market.

Wright

While preparing for this interview, I read that the first film in your series titled, *The Business of Paradigms*™ is the best-selling business film of all time. Is that true?

Christensen

Yes.

Wright

My goodness!

Christensen

Yes. That was first created in the '80s by the futurist, Joel Barker, and my father. It's been translated in many, many languages. FISH! is creeping up there, though. It's going to surpass *The Business Paradigms* someday.

Wright

When you speak and train, how do you motivate people to create workplaces that are joyful and innovative, lighthearted and wholehearted?

Christensen

The interesting part of all this is when we tell them about it and they see the film or read the book. There's something that connects inside them that says either they had this in them or they were searching for this—this lightheartedness—this engagement of being at work and being engaged in what you do.

We've made a film series with a poet named David White. David talks about being wholehearted. He has a friend—a monk—who said, "The way around burnout isn't necessarily burnout. It's being wholehearted in what you do." Now that's incredible. That means is, if you come to work and you're totally engaged and enjoy what you are doing, the day goes by much quicker and you're going to be connected to it.

Wright

Do you find many CEOs, or especially upper management people, that are a little—

Christensen

Apprehensive of this?

Wright

Yes.

Christensen

Yes, there are. But for the corporations that embrace it and "get it," stand back—watch out for their organizations!

For instance, the CEO of Aspen Ski Co., a ski company in Aspen, Colorado, who has embraced it said, "This is the pull; this is what we're going to be. This is the way we're going to service our employees. We're going to be engaged with what we do." They have 3,500 seasonal employees. They teach them every year. They teach them the FISH! Philosophy when the new group comes in, or even when part of the old group comes back in. They resurface the philosophy and say, "Remember—be engaged." When they open that playing field and give them the boundaries of saying, "Okay, safety is first in any business; here are the playing fields. Be safe. Don't do anything that's rude or crude," they see things happening.

For example, a young man created his own super hero called "Captain Iowa." He'd "fly" kids through the lift line up to the front and he'd help create an atmosphere that was "engaging." It distracted people when they were standing there for twenty-five minutes waiting for their turn on the ski lift. They also started karaoke in the waiting lines, and they do limbo. Now, that created an atmosphere because, again, the CEO is saying, "Look, we have great snow and the same mountains as the other resorts. What separates us from the other ski resort businesses?" The difference was the way they engaged with customers.

That's the way, first and foremost, to have people engage in their work and be happy with where they are. I'm not just talking about making a "Pollyannaish" happy, happy workplace. I'm talking about people being engaged in what they do. Now, if you have that and you create that kind of atmosphere, watch out! Your bottom line is going to go up and your employee turnover is going to go down.

Another thing we find that's just really amazing is, when you step back and analyze it, we're in our places of work more than we are in our places of worship, more than we are in the great outdoors, and more than we are with our families. Now, if we can't connect to that, be engaged, and take joy in what we're doing, that's a sad commentary on our life. What are you giving up your hours for? What are you spending your life's energy on? What are you giving, where are you giving your energy—your life energy to? Is this the place you really want to be? Is this the place that's going to make you flourish?

Wright

What do you mean by "make their day?" Are these management theories that apply to employees, or are these employee theories that apply to customers?

Christensen

It applies absolutely to everyone. It's employee-to-employee, it's employer-to-employee, and it's employee-to-customer. It's the whole thing. I'm saying is coming to work with that attitude realizing your life is about what you are giving to people. "Make their day" is just a new term of saying it—make people's day.

Serving others is when we really find joy. It doesn't matter if the CEO is talking to a vice-president or a president, or if an employee is talking to a guest in a hotel, the philosophy is make people's day! And it doesn't take much. The stories we hear about the little nuances of what makes people's day are amazing. I mean, just being with a person moves us into "being there." What does "being there" mean? It means just being in the moment with a person.

For example, if you're trying to talk to somebody in your office and you've got the phone ringing and a message coming in on your cell phone, put it all away. Let voicemail answer the phone, put the cell phone away, and really be there with the person. When you're in the presence of a person, he or she can feel it.

Do I have time to share a story with you?

Wright

Sure.

Christensen

There was a prison guard who was in the service area of a jail; he was the "booking agent," shall we say. The police department he worked for went through the FISH! Philosophy teaching, and he became aware of being present and making people's day. The prison guard was totally in the moment with a shoplifter, who was being booked for shoplifting. He gave the person dignity and respect. The prisoner started to weep, saying, "I've never been treated this way in my life, much less I'm being booked for a crime I know I did." That's being present. The prison guard made that guy's day! It might have made a huge difference in that guy's life too, maybe—who knows?

FISH! brings to the surface what people have in them. It gives them a way to say, "I can do this—I have permission. My organization has shown me the light of being a 'day-maker'."

Be private with people. When you're choosing your attitude, making people's day, and being present for people, guess what? The appropriate "play" comes out.

Wright

In reference to the third principle, "choose your attitude," we're publishing a book for a man now about attitude. One of his favorite sayings is, "The difference between a good day and a bad day is your attitude."

Christensen

Absolutely. We all have magnificent stories about our lives. But if you look at people who have tragedies in some respect, and they come to work whistling, what is that? How would we face some of these tragedies if they happened to us? That is what we mean by "choose your attitude."

Wright

John, I'd like to quote something you said referring to business. The quote is: "We need people who are passionate, committed, and free to live the organization's vision through their personal value." Would you explain what you were talking about?

Christensen

Yes. When you have an alignment with what you stand for as an individual and what the company—the organization—is standing for, step out of the way. Watch out! Watch the power that happens with that.

Wright

When you talk about businesses, you use words like "love" and "soul."

Christensen

Right.

Wright

Most people would think that spiritual values would not be appropriate in a business setting. Do companies accept your spiritual values as necessary ingredients to success?

Christensen

There's a whole new movement out there about spirituality. I want it to be clear—we're not talking religion. We're talking about the spirit and soul of people and these elements bring the soul of a business alive.

We made a film with Southwest Airlines. Herb Kelleher and Rollin King founded Southwest Airlines stating, "We wanted to create a workplace based on love rather than fear." Now, if Southwest Airlines with 33,000 employees is based on love and is doing incredibly well in the airline industry as of this writing, is that not a valuable statement to everybody in business?

Wright

Is there anything or anyone in your life who has made a difference for you and helped you to become a better person?

Christensen

I have a lot of mentors in my life. My parents have been incredible mentors. My mom was a social worker and a very incredible people-oriented woman. My dad was an artist. Combined, they have been wonderful mentors for me. I've also had the blessing of having Ken Blanchard as a mentor and Spencer Johnson, so I've had great mentors in that respect, too.

Wright

I was talking to Jim Cathcart the other day. I told him that one of my mentors had no knowledge of his being a mentor—Bill Gove from Florida. I have been listening to his talks and tapes and reading his books for probably forty years.

What do you think makes up a mentor? In other words, are there characteristics that mentors seem to have in common?

Christensen

I believe they're different for everybody. I mean everybody finds a different mentor. I think some of the most beautiful mentorships happen when a person takes you under their wing.

Another inspiration for me is Norman Vincent Peale. Okay, he's got religion in there, but his books and writings were a type of mentorship for me. His presence, the way he spoke so eloquently with so much passion mentored me.

Many different things can inspire you. If a tape or a book inspires you and that tool becomes your mentor—fabulous. When it opens you up to the possibilities in your life, whether it is a book, a personal relationship, a tape, a film, these are all wonderful aspects of opening you up to possibilities.

Wright

I remember when I was in Seattle a few years ago and saw the people working in the fish company you wrote about. I remember two feelings about them. One was a feeling that this would be a nice place to buy something; but the biggest feeling was that these guys are really happy and having fun. And they've got a tough job too—it's not the kind of job a bank president would have.

Christensen

No. Hey, they don't work in air conditioning and heating. They work with dead fish, ice, and cold cement floors. I've wiped out there many a time. It's just showing you the possibilities when workers like they are can practice these principles successfully with their hands in dead fish, ice, during twelve-hour days. That's what's so powerful about it. That's why we call it the FISH! Philosophy. It's based on the fact that if fish market workers can do it, you can do it. The philosophy comes from ancient wisdom and was noticed as a practice among sellers in that fish market. If folks in a fish market can do it, we can all do it.

Wright

We've talked about three out of four of the principles. The last one I'd like to ask you about is the principle "be there." Do you mean come to work on time and be there? Or be there for people?

Christensen

Be there for people. I mean, absolutely be in the moment. As I was saying, when you're with somebody, put the other things down. I catch myself so many times sitting at my desk when people come in, and I'm reading something at the time. I'm just half with them. You have to take that moment and put what you're doing down and be there for them.

Another good little exercise to do is when the phone rings; take a moment before you pick it up and just pause. Think about what you're going to do on the phone. It doesn't matter if it's a salesperson or whomever; just remember to be there in the moment when you're on the phone with a person. It's an interesting little exercise of being present.

Wright

Most people are fascinated with these new television programs about being a survivor. What has been the greatest comeback you have made from adversity in your career or in your life?

Christensen

Wow! The biggest adversity? Well, there are two. We went through a stint with a company where some people tried to take over our business, and I made it through that. But one of the things was living up to my mentor's—my father's—image and having knowing in my heart and in my gut that I had the capacity to lead the company and to be a great filmmaker like my father. And I don't mean great in a cocky way—I'm saying bringing what we bring to the table of documentaries and showing the world what the possibilities are. That's what I mean by "great." That was a high; but it was a hurdle to work through also.

Wright

When I was researching for this interview, I noticed on your Web site they also referred to Joel Barker, the futurist who helped your father, was also referred to.

Christensen

Futurist, correct.

Wright

And so your father started making what? Documentary films?

Christensen

Yes. He started off in advertising just when television was getting started in the late '50s. He happened to be in love with the documentary approach. He pursued the documentarian lifestyle and would go off and make films. What he brought to the table was this uniqueness—this anthropological aspect of looking at something, studying it, and saying, "What can we do to show that?"

For instance, when his career started off in Omaha, Nebraska, he made a film about the city of Omaha. But through the whole film, you didn't know where you were until the end of the film, *Come See Our City, Omaha*. But it showed you who the people were, what the organizations were like in Omaha, and it persuaded you that you'd like to come and live there and build your business there. So he brought that approach to it (i.e., let's study it, let's bring it; let's show people what it's about instead of telling them.

That's what happened with the paradigm idea—let's look at a paradigm in all these different ways. If it doesn't get you this way, look at it another way. If this story doesn't connect with you, look at it another way, then perhaps you can relate to *that* way.

Wright

The freewheeling workplace of the 1990s is long gone. Companies are cutting perks. Employees are reverting from casual attire to business wear. How can employees really "play" at work when the reins are being pulled back so tightly?

Christensen

Well, that's our point—the reigns shouldn't be pulled back so tightly. Ken Blanchard calls it the "tight underwear syndrome." We need to get rid of that. We need to free people up because when you're free is when creativity and innovation happens. I don't know where the quote comes from, but it was said, "If 'work' was 'play,' Silicon Valley would not have been created." Two guys in their garage—Bill Hewlett and Dave Packard—I mean, how many guys were in their garage "playing" and tinkering around, right? And they came up with the Hewlett-Packard audio oscillator and went on to make computers, printers, etc. The Apple computer was Steven Wozniak's first contribution to the personal computer field. I mean, how many more can we list? These folks were playing and came up with some of the most innovative ideas in their field!

Back to the original idea, it's the playfulness—how we saw the fishmongers reacting to each other and reacting to customers at the fish market. You see what they're doing and make your own style based on that. It opens you up to saying, "What can *we* do that's about playfulness?"

Wright

I've heard about the impact that FISH! is having on corporate America. Has it been used outside the business world?

Wright

Schools are among our biggest clientele. It's amazing! We're now creating a curriculum for schools and we're working on creating how to interpret this and bring into the classroom. If you could talk about "play," "being present," "choose your attitude," and "make people's day" with elementary students, imagine what possibilities lie in the future for that!

Wright

Are you having more success getting it into the private schools or public schools?

Christensen

Public schools are embracing it. First and foremost right now, what's happening is that administrators and teachers are being brought into discussions about how we can engage them with their work. It goes back to discovering what kind of organization we can be and how we're going to help people be engaged in what we're here for, whether the business is a hospital, a school, or a manufacturing plant.

We worked with a roofing company that used this philosophy and it turned their entire company around. Now they're a world famous roofing company; they get roofing jobs in different places throughout the world. How did they do this? They changed their philosophy and became more effective in how they do business.

Now, back to education and using this philosophy in the classroom. If you are a teacher being present in the classroom for your kids—they're the customers, you have to serve them.

How about your partner? He or she is there to teach you as much as you are there to teach him or her. My goodness! I mean, that was my first love—I wanted to be a teacher asking, "What can you bring to the table?"

The kind of teacher we need is like the English professor, John Keating, in the film *Dead Poets Society.* We need teachers who are engaged with the minds of our youth asking, "How do I get to them? How do I reach them? How am I there with them? What do I do to make their day?"

We're actually working on the concept of saying the four principles of FISH! are the rules of the classroom by asking questions like, "What am I doing today to play—to be playful?" This works both ways. This is teacher-to-student and partner-to-partner philosophy. What are we doing to make the classroom fun? What are we doing to make each other's day? How am I being there for you? How are you being there for me? How are you being there for your other your peers? And first and foremost, how are you choosing to come to school? How are you choosing to "be here" today—what is your attitude?

Wright

Very interesting. Boy, this has been a fast, fast thirty minutes. I really do appreciate your being a guest today on *Bootstrap Business*. I really appreciate the time you've taken to answer these questions.

Christensen

Well, David, thank you, and thanks for helping to spread the word.

Wright

Today we have been talking with John Christensen whose story began, as he said, working with his father who is a great role model for him. You've heard how the FISH! Philosophy can literally change you and your company's future, as it's changing the future for many companies in America.

I'd like to shamelessly advertise the book; I think everyone should read it. I know you're making good at Amazon.com. Can people get it directly from you or can they find out more on your Web site? If you'll give us that information, I would appreciate it.

Christensen

Absolutely. It is available at www.charthouse.com. On the site you can go to fishphilosophy.com, which is an entire Web site with all the FISH! information. You can purchase our films as well as our ancillary products, our fishing gear, and you can purchase the books. Now there are two books on the market, David. There's *First Fish!* and our second book that came out called *Fish Tales*.

Wright

I hope our readers will rush to the Web site and get this book. I've got *Fish Tales*, I'm going to get the first one.

Christensen

Thank you, David. Thank you so much. I really appreciate your time.

ABOUT THE AUTHOR

John Christensen's story begins in the shipping department at ChartHouse Learning where he began working as a teenager for his father, Ray. He worked his way to the top the old-fashioned way, proving to his father—and the company—that he was a real filmmaker who could tell moving stories. Today Christensen guides ChartHouse as "Playground Director" (CEO in business-speak) with an inspiring vision of an engaged workplace that can be developed through the FISH! Philosophy. The rest of the story is that ChartHouse Learning is changing the way business is done worldwide.

Like his dad before him, John has created an eloquent language to transform lives. In 1998 he translated what happens daily at Seattle's world famous Pike Place Fish Market's culture into a viable, global learning program called FISH! And changed the entire business film industry. In the process, John also achieved his lifelong dream of how to turn workplaces into energetic, creative, and wholehearted endeavors with the four simple principles embodied in the FISH! Philosophy: Play, Make their Day, Be There, and Choose Your Attitude.

Today John speaks to vastly different organizations about his journey—the serendipitous discovery of the fish market—and how that simple FISH! Philosophy he and his team poetically articulated on film four years ago can dramatically change the stories of companies and individuals.

John Christensen

www.charthouse.com

www.fishphilopophy.com

CHAPTER TWELVE

An interview with...

Dr. William W. Kenner

Quantum Communications: Reaching the Subconscious

David Wright (Wright)

Today we're talking with Dr. William Kenner, a Doctor of medical Hypnotherapy, Divinity, and Metaphysics. He is also a professor of Communications for the University of Michigan and is a professional trainer and coach and training specialist for "Quantum Communications: Reaching Your Subconscious Mind."

We all somehow "know" that the mind/body connection is key to better communication and business. So many are tired of trying to find the words that describe how business will work in the future with the balance of a world linking relationships of body, mind, and spirit, and why their relationships are so important for business and communication. William has researched a renaissance in cell biology and subconscious processing and communication that provides the cutting edge for this new science of creativity, change, and leadership. This is real science that has proven how twenty-first century communication skills are biologically and psychologically evolving. Research is the foundation to this paradigm shift in the biology and psychology of subconscious communication. This new and exciting science will inspire your spirit, engage your mind, and challenge your creativity, as you comprehend the enormous real potential for applying this information in life, learning, and discovering your inner strengths.

William, welcome to *Bootstrap Business.*

Kenner

Thank you. I am honored.

Wright

What is "quantum communication"?

Kenner

The word "quantum" comes from the Latin neuter of *quantus*—literally "how great." It means a unit of quantity. Quantum mechanics refers to the energy of an atom at rest. Atomic and subatomic systems are called quantum mechanics. Quantum mechanics gave order to a system of information that appeared to be in chaos.

Wright

Why the shift to quantum mechanics in human communications?

Kenner

Quantum mechanics were developed to provide a better explanation of the atom when Newtonian physics failed. Newtonian physics validated law and order, but what about the space in between? Does it not have information as well? Quantum communication is the study of the space in between the conscious and subconscious minds that allow authentic quantum communication to occur.

Wright

Is there an example of this that could help to explain the idea that all information as energy?

Kenner

In the communication process, all information can simply be defined as energy in a system that flows from sender to receiver. The information moves from sender to receiver and communication occurs. In the Newtonian physics world, communication would look like Figure 1:

Newtonian—Linear Flow of Information

INFORMATION FLOW

A ➡ B ➡ C ➡ D ➡ E

Figure 1

The change in quantum communication allows for more energy to flow in multiple directions simultaneously. The flow in communication simultaneous from multiple senders and receivers and is very transactional—a person is always sending and receiving energy. It would look like Figure 2:

Quantum—Holistic Flow of Information

INFORMATION FLOW

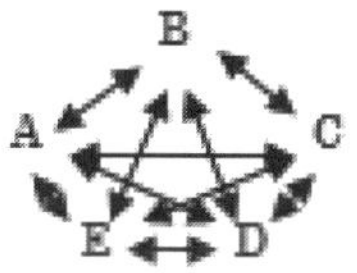

Figure 2

Wright

When you look at information to include the space in between, it appears as if the division of the information actually creates more information. Will you describe that a bit more?

Kenner

Every thought, every feeling, every attitude, every emotion, every action is information and is energy. "What you do with that informational energy, affects your life in every way" (Myss, 2002 p. 42).

As a sample, this graphic is a simple example of the wave pattern information for the Newtonian science of light. We know that what human eyes can see in light waves is simple RGB (red, green, blue) science. This is a fraction of the total information content for the topic of light. How much more information about light exists to the right of the RGB light spectrum?

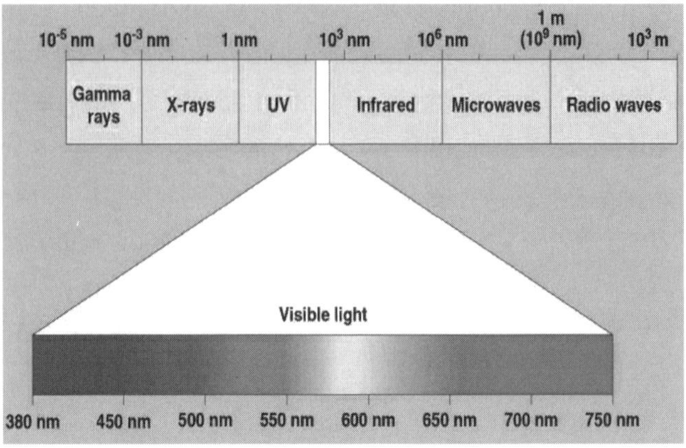

Quantum information exists beyond what you can see, hear, feel, taste, or touch. It is the information of perception. Scientifically, we know much more, such as data about light that is infrared energy, microwaves, radio waves, etc. How many more different vibration levels exist to the right (higher vibrations) of those in the illustration? Infinite numbers! What about the left (lower vibrations) of the RGB light spectrum? We have UV rays, X-rays, Gamma rays, etc. Again, how much more exists to the left of those? Infinite!

Wright

This is ground-breaking information. Where did you begin understanding this connection to human communication and business?

Kenner

As the study in human hypnosis becomes more and more applied to the science of changing human behaviors, the research had to visit the space where subconscious communication takes place. Business and industry has been using hypnosis in multiple forms for centuries to increase motivation, productivity, and achievement. When the business world finally gave space to allow for the perceptions that affect the receptors of the communicator and leader, we began to see ideas like the tipping point, seeds of innovation, and authentic group processes for change. It is communication at a cellular level. If your organization is one or one million, every thought and action a person has contributes to communication, and learning affects that organization. Affirmations (positive or negative) actually do affect us biologically. We qualify our energy with our own thoughts. The self-talk matters—thinking good, positive thoughts and not destructive, defeating thoughts changes the energy of information in communication.

Wright

Western science has long ignored descriptions of energetic components of physiology because their existence could never be documented by dissection or viewed under a microscope. How has this changed?

Kenner

It is only through the acceptance of this multidimensional framework of the human energy field of quantum physics that scientists and business has begun to comprehend the true nature of human physiology in communication, business, and cellular change.

Figure 3 demonstrates that all information must go through the part of the mind called the "critical faculties." It is then stored in the subconscious mind only if the information is in agreement with what is previously stored or if it is the first time the information has been received. If either of these is true, then the information goes into the subconscious automatically. Using the psychological theory of the law of compounding, if the information is supported three times with matching information, the information is then moved into permanent memory. The dilemma is "the subconscious cannot judge" (Parkhill, 1996, p. 121).

Human communication has evolved into something that has several connective layers within the conscious, subconscious, and unconscious minds. Figure three helps to explain this concept.

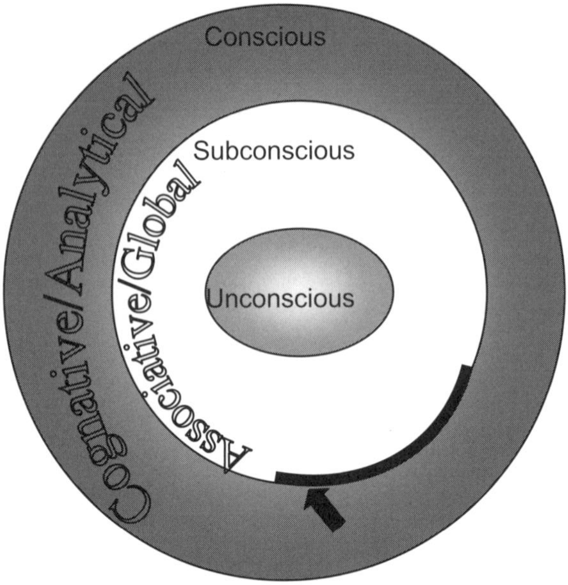

As long as our rational mind can come up with reasons for our actions, our "critical judgment" will keep us at peace. Willpower (cognitive judgment) cannot effect internal (associative) change. The subconscious mind works to achieve the perceived self-image.

If there is nothing to judge against, there can be no critical faculty. All information must pass through this "gate" called the critical faculties. If prior information is stored, it is compared and is either accepted or rejected based on currently stored "truths." If nothing is stored on this topic, then the gate remains open to take in new data. If compounded three times, it is then "accepted" and is then stored into long-term memory.

If you want to watch the evolutionary emergence of a new species, look in the mirror. Zukav (1999) said that the entire human species is in the midst of a great evolutionary transformation. Humans have the potential to become a more highly intuitive species. Humans are emerging as multi-sensory information gatherers from the old system of power-driven receivers. At the heart of Zukav's perspective is his belief that:

"Human evolution is becoming a connection between the conscious and subconscious minds. We're co-creators in our own evolution. External power—manipulating, dominating, and controlling the physical world—is not 'bad,' it is obsolete, the source of violence and destruction." (Zukav, p. 16).

Zukav says he is pragmatic. He believes creating authentic power is a day-to-day, moment-by-moment endeavor in which people must make choices and then be responsible for the outcome of those choices. There's no place here for blaming others or for acting the part of the victim. Zukav does not propose that this transformation is easy.

"The five-sensory human was a stage. It's past. We now have a new potential to align our physical and spiritual selves. We can choose to create this multi-sensory human, or not. It's our choice. We get to choose what we create and co-create. This transformation is about living a life. Become uniquely who you are. Becoming aware of how you feel, then speaking the truth about those feelings. Detach from the outcome of having spoken the truth. It is hard work to be responsible and it's the reason you were born" (Zukav, p. 18).

Wright

These thoughts are a revolutionary perspective! As the light spectrum illustration in the beginning of this discussion demonstrated, we can begin to see that as human evolve into energy understanding machines, they are also able to take in the perception that infinite unknown information can be something that must be acknowledged outside of what you can merely see, hear, feel taste or touch.

Kenner

Business communication and developing creativity and twenty-first century business practices are not a mathematical equation. We are dealing with organic, evolving humans in a constant state of change and chaos. Positive and negative thought (perceptions) affect the body and mind as a whole. You are what you think. When Christopher Columbus sailed to the Americas his ships could not be seen by the Native Americans. They had no grounding visualization in their experience to know what the objects were, so their minds simply erased it from existence. Stored subconscious perceptions may create a diluted perception of reality. Perception is the process of attaining awareness or understanding of multi-sensory information that creates the reality of human strength.

Wright

What do we need to do to become better human communicators to pull up the bootstraps of business?

Kenner

We need to not worship the evaluation process of business communication. It does not take into account the internal change that is required for external change. Just like anything in the study of communication, the process of implementation and evaluation needs to be a living, breathing process. Think of evaluation as a tool rather than the final word. "The survival and thriving of our species will depend on our nurturing of potentials that are distinctly human" (Gardner, 2006, p. 167). This is a great shift from the business communication practices of the past built on economy and economics. The place where business communicators will meet is the space in between. This is where discoveries of inner strengths begin.

Leaders, coaches, supervisors, trainers, and even floor workers must develop a program to educate the individual on all levels of the body, mind, and spirit. The subconscious is where these informational energies will meet to discuss or discover strengths and weaknesses of a business to either move forward in change or wear down the mechanics of individuality with an inability to see the space in between.

Subconscious communication is an energy science affecting the subconscious perceptions for authentic physical change. The cells of the body require active subconscious involvement of the person requesting discovery or change. "Cells generally respond to an assortment of very basic perceptions of what's going on in their world . . . the simultaneous interactions of tens of thousands of reflective perceptions switches in the membrane, each directly reading an individual environment signal, collectively create the behavior of a living cell" (Lipton, 2005, p. 129).

Wright

As old models that no longer work give way to the new ones, we are left to weave the old patterns of higher order thinking and business into forms that fit our new understanding of multisensory business and change. Are there any thoughts or ideas that can help with this process?

Kenner

"You want to reach a critical mass of advocates so that the change reaches a tipping point and people flow naturally into the advocate pool" (Shapiro, 2004, p. 93). It is time for everyone to jump into the pool of the space in between conscious and subconscious communication and discover their own inner strengths.

Wright

What a great conversation this has been. Thank you for such an in-depth subject but how simply you were able to help with how discovering an inner strength really happens.

Kenner

Thank you. It has been my pleasure and I look forward to more information to come in the future.

Wright

Today we have been talking with Dr. William Kenner, a professional trainer, educator, and researcher on human communication and business and the power of the subconscious mind and human behavior.

William, thank you for your help in *Bootstrap Business* and the information about how we are evolving human beings and how this will affect business leadership, creativity, and innovation.

References

Gardner, H. (2006). *Five minds for the future*. Boston: Harvard Business School Press.

Lipton, B. (2005). *The biology of belief: Unleashing the power of consciousness, matter and miracles.* Sana Rosa, CA: Mountain of Love.

Myss, C. (1997). *Anatomy of the spirit: The seven stages of power and healing*. Kalamazoo, MI: Three Rivers Press.

Parkhill, Stephen C. (1995). *Answer cancer*. Fort Lauderdale: Omni Hypnosis Publishing.

Pulus, L. (2004). *The biology of empowerment*. Niles, IL : Nightingale Conant. Audio Program.

Zukav, G. (1999). *The seat of the soul*. New York: Simon & Schuster.

ABOUT THE AUTHOR

Dr. William W. Kenner has been working in education, psychology, business, and performing arts for more than twenty-two years. William is a Doctor of Medical Hypnotherapy, Divinity, and Metaphysics, and a Master of Arts in Education. He teaches and consults as a medical hypnotherapist, and an education and business professional development trainer. He is currently completing his dissertation for a PhD in Education. William's professional accomplishments and abilities are as eclectic as his education. He is a lecturer for the University of Michigan Flint, and adjunct faculty member for St. Clair County Community College, Michigan. With a very busy schedule of keynote and workshop presentations in education, business, industry, psychology, health and healing, and performing arts, William has traveled the world with his lectures on "Quantum Communication and Teaching: Reaching the Subconscious Mind." He has been honored by several national educational, community, business, and arts organizations for helping gifted and at-risk populations.

Dr. William W. Kenner

Medical Hypnotherapist and Professional Development Trainer
2809 Peavey Street
Port Huron, MI 48060
810.388.0539 (Office)
586.256.5822 (Cellular)
wwkenner@comcast.net (Office e-mail)
wwkenner@umflint.edu (University e-mail)
www.ThisIsASquare.com